Corey and Patrick's Crap-a-Pedia

Written & Edited By
Corey Deitz and Patrick Beam

Personalized Autograph Suggestions

In the event you are able to obtain autographs from the authors, this page has been set aside to help "personalize" the experience!

To our dear friend_____
It's always a pleasure to see you!
Best Regards,

We don't know you, but _____
Said you would enjoy this book!
Best Regards,

Table of Contents

Dedications 7

Foreword 8

If Pygmies Made the Shakes at Fast Food
Restaurants 10

A Short History of Men Cooking 12

Dropping Deuces and Floating Air Biscuits 18

Fire: The Original 22

Ever Had a Colonoscopy? Patrick's Preparation
Journal 25

Man vs. Time 30

Science Is Gonna' Make Your Poop Smell Good . 32

Man vs. Time 34

Bad Idea #7,346 35

Man vs. Time 37

Doctor, I have 40

Man vs. Time 42

Man vs. Time 44

A Short History of Men Grilling 47

Corey's Meatloaf Burger 50

Men and Health – A Pictorial 51

Corey's Turkey Burgers That Don't Taste Like Shit
.... 59

The Good, the Bad, and the Moldy 61

Man Fears: Zombies 63

Spontaneous Vocabulary 66

The Food Police 69

One Day at God's Desk 71

The Church of Bacon 73

I'm a Food Separatist 75

Is that a Dildo in Your Happy Meal?....................76
A Short History of 78
Whiny Food Bitches 80
Man Pisses Away Earth 83
Fast Food Felons...86
The Green Police 88
Pizza Continues to be Abused – and we do Nothing!
....90
The Man Who Tattooed a Radio Station Logo to
His Forehead..92
Who Put the Doom in the *Doom-De-Doom-De-
Doom?*...95
You are *Already*..98
Food of the Gods: 100
Get Your Odor Motor Running 102
The Moment Corey was Diagnosed with Depression
....104
Meysken's Drunk as Shit Chili 106
The Edible Mist Machine 107
You Cannot Lose Weight Through Osmosis.......109
Church of the Intelligent Robot 111
What if Jesus had been Fat?..............................113
Grateful for Dead Tech....................................114
Long Live Penmanship!....................................116
Man vs. Animals: How Much Competition do you
Want?..119
Earthling: Take Me to Your Latte! 121
Starbucks Euphemisms for Masturbation............125
Man Conquers Space 126
The Great Debate:..127
One Day at the Cheese Oracle 129

Please, Don't Send Me There 131
The Worst Condiment..133
A Short History of Condiments 134
In Grill We Trust 140
Why Do We Say That?..143
Why Do We Say That?..145
Why Men Love the #10 Can...............................147
T-Rex Sex 149
Man vs. Toaster 151
Rats! Another Bomb!..154
~~Men~~ Infants at Work..156
A Short History of Cats 158
Suck it, Turtle! 162
Dude, Your Breath Smells Like a Gym...............164
We like our Hamburgers......................................166
Church's Donation Plate Replaced with Panties! 169
What if God Had a Facebook Page?....................171
The Balls Are in Her Court..................................173
The Truth is *Really* 175
'Pot' Still Legal for Lobsters 177
A Short History of Yogurt 179
Author Acknowledgement...................................182
Books by Corey Deitz...183

Dedications

To my sons, Noah and Tyler. Now you can officially say. "Dad is full of crap." – Patrick Beam

To my partner, Parick Beam: "I knew that already!" – Corey Deitz

Foreword

Eating, sleeping, and pooping. That's what we do. Generally, eating is its own distraction and few of us tend to need a book during a meal. If you are reading while sleeping, then you are amazing and you will think the crass tripe in this volume is beneath you. So leave now. For the rest of you, the majority of poopers, we say welcome!

This is a bathroom reader. Bathroom readers are so popular bookstores have a complete category just for them. Apparently, the world agrees that the involuntary process of elimination is so boring, we must do something even our parents and teachers couldn't convince us to do: read!

The difference between this bathroom reader and every single other reader comes down to who do you want as a bathroom companion? Do you want a book authored by some stranger? Some "smarty pants" author who has jumbled book full of random fact together OR would you rather spend time on the toilet accompanied by two men who you are very familiar with?

This book is a compilation of humorous and entertaining material all written by Corey Deitz and Patrick Beam or "Corey and Patrick in the Monring." Some of it has been expertly extracted from on-air conversations, on-air bits, regularly scheduled segments like "Patrick's Weekly Rant" or in Corey's case, previous books and articles that lent themselves to this project. In addition, there is a lot of original material which has been created just for Crap-a-Pedia. You will know who contributed what particular piece by the initials at the end of a particular entry:

- PB stands for Patrick Beam
- CD stands for Corey Deitz

Occasionally, you might see both initials which signify a joint contribution.

In addition, independent contributors will be identified clearly. There is no particular way to read this book. The contents were compiled in a random way so you can open it anywhere and just begin. Should you need more formality, there is a table of contents.

We hope you enjoy this book and encourage you to buy many copies for anyone else who has demonstrated the behavior of pooping! Please see the next page for personalized autograph suggestions! – CD

If Pygmies Made the Shakes at Fast Food Restaurants

Worker on speaker: *Welcome to Puny's where every meal cost a small fortune. How can I help you?*

Corey: *I'd like a shake please.*

Worker on speaker: *Our shake machine is broken today but good news: the pygmies have punched in.*

Corey: *What does that mean?*

Worker on speaker: *That means the pygmies are going to duct tape blenders to their asses and mix your shake personally!*

Corey: *Isn't that a health code violation?*

Worker on speaker: *No, sir. Our pygmies have had their shots and have been de-wormed.*

Corey: *You make them sound like dogs.*

Worker on speaker: *They definitely are as cute as doggies! Now, what flavor would you like?*

Corey: *Chocolate.*

Worker on speaker: *Sorry, we can't serve chocolate today. The pygmies believe this is a strawberry-only day. They are very superstitious. They usually pray in the morning to a wooden totem pole that's decorated with the faces of the Gods. The pole tells them what flavors are proper for each day.*

Corey: *Look, I don't believe in their totem pole. Why do I have to feel the brunt of this?*

Worker on speaker: *Because, sir, if you annoy the pygmies they will shoot you with poison darts and then grill you up on a spit large enough to hold a bison.*

Corey: *I'd like to change my order. Just a small fry.*

Worker on speaker: *Is that some sort of pygmy insult? (off mike) We need some darts up front...*
- CD

A Short History of Men Cooking

Men started cooking after they discovered fire, about 125,000 B.C. - Before Cooking.

Fire changed everything which is why today's male continues to salute his forefathers by lighting up backyard grills and cooking the shit out of anything that once mooed, oinked, quacked, or clucked.

Before fire, there was only occasional and random cooking which happened solely by accident - like when a lightning bolt would strike a Wooly Mammoth and set it on fire. Nothing whets the appetite like seeing an elephant-like creature running through the forest lit up like a Tiki Torch. Yes, that was a big "yum" for early man.

Burnt Wooly Mammoth became such a delicacy that eventually Neanderthals decided they needed to harness the power of fire. Unfortunately, the first few attempts were futile and deadly. For instance, man - Neanderthals - or whoever was there – soon learned that it was an extremely bad idea to stand in an open field during a thunderstorm in order to become a human fire stick. Though it was relatively easy to get struck by lightning, the real problem was trying to avoid being burned alive while running back to the rest of the tribe with your chest hairs on fire. This was eventually deemed an inefficient way to transfer a spark from your body to pile of sticks on the ground.

Thus, it was bittersweet.

Early man had fire in his hands – literally – but, had no way of controlling it. So, for a long time man had to be content with Steak Tartare. (Oddly, today, you can still enjoy that dish but you'll have to pay through the nose at a 5-star restaurant. Sometimes, you just don't know how good you have it!)

In Early times, Men Had to Coax Beef to Slaughter by Playing Song by the group, Slayer

Anyway, back to fire.

The first man to use a grill with fire was Moses. Many are familiar with the story of Moses encountering the burning bush on Mt. Horeb. The story is widely recounted in the Book of Exodus in the Old Testament. Actually, the burning bush was also the first Weber grill. Yes, Weber is a nice Jewish name. When God made the burning bush appear to Moses, the old man reached into his carry pack and instinctively pulled out some a couple of steaks. He immediately tossed them on top of the burning bush and the first instance of charbroil occurred.

Don't doubt me on this.

In the Middle Ages, Knights of the Roundtable often relaxed on a Saturday by catching a fire-breathing dragon and tying it to a tree. They would then invite their friend over and grill fresh meat and toast marshmallows. I can assure you, nothing taste quite like a marshmallow that has been toasted from the flame of a dragon's nostril!

Naturally, there were a few drawbacks to using dragon fire to cook over a flame – like being burned alive if the dragon got loose from its chains or when somebody accidentally tripped over the butter pail on lobster night, allowing flammable liquid to completely torch half the village.

In the 1700s, America's famous statesman, Benjamin Franklin, was often invited to parties because people loved to watch him harness electricity with a kite in order to start barbecues with a lightning strike. Few know that the first instance of barbecued ribs actually belonged to a human who got a bit too close to Franklin one summer night.

But, despite the accidents, death, destruction, and fear, cooking over fire continued to be a favorite way for people to make their food taste better.

Few people know today that during the 1800s, especially in America, a fashionable trend came along called "mini-cooking." The challenge was to cook a complete 7-course meal for 20 people using only a thimble and a candle. Mini-cooking was all the rage as parties which often started on a Saturday night and ended 3 months later. Though some party guests survived, generally everyone invited starved to death prior to desert. Mini-cooking eventually faded as the zeitgeist of the times but, the authors are somewhat excited that we were able to use the word "zeitgeist" in this book since there are few opportunities to do so exist these days.

Mankind and cooking continued to flourish into the 20th Century as stoves evolved from wood-fueled to gas-fueled and eventually in the 1930s, electric-fueled. The first electric stove was manufactured by the rock band, AC/DC and came

Rocky Mountain Oysters, or Bull Testicles, are a Delicacy Men Love! Unless Something Goes Horribly Wrong!

with 10 free pounds of young, Angus steak. The *High Voltage* and *Powerage* from the electricity was available at the *Flick of a Switch*. Each stove came with a personal note from the president of the company which began, "*For Those About to ~~Rock~~ Cook, We Salute You!*"

Microwave ovens appeared in the late 1940s but were very large at first. Initially, they were only used in cooking live, whole cows. PETA, the People for Eating Toasted Angus, thought this was a great idea.

It wasn't until 1967, when a company called Amana Corporation, introduced a microwave model small enough to conveniently fit in a typical kitchen. It immediately caused the Angus beef markets to crash and lowered the price of live cows substantially. But, the smaller microwave signaled a leap in mankind's cooking preparations and allowed us to remove dangerous substances like fire and gas from our kitchen in favor of faster microwaves that could penetrate your organs and give you radiation sickness.

In conclusion, man's quest for decent food that doesn't taste like the underside of a muddy boot has been a long and hard struggle. Through advancements, technology, trial, error, and a great amount of booze, we have found ourselves at the edge of a new culinary frontier.

God help us!

- CD

Dropping Deuces and Floating Air Biscuits

The Danger of Co-Shitting

I once worked for a business financing company with about 120 employees. It was a typical, white collar environment in the downtown area of Little Rock. One day at lunch, a buddy and I were in the middle of a bitchfest about our bathroom situation.

ME: "Man, I hate when I have to take a dump because, inevitably, someone always sits down in the stall next to me and I freeze up"

BUDDY: DUDE! Me, too! I have to try to wait it out til they leave! It sucks. "

This is where it went wrong.

ME: "Dude! Let's co-shit!"

BUDDY: "Huh?"

ME: " If we go in at the same time, we can both take care of our business and be embarrassed."

BUDDY: "That's brilliant! I'm all in"

Now, at first it may sound really gay but it's not. You could call it "bromo" but not "homo" because we didn't wanna' hook up. We just wanted safe passage to the poopski. We agreed to call each other and give a ten minute warning. It worked flawlessly for months until tragedy struck.

My buddy called to sound the heinous anus alarm. I said I would be there in five minutes. What I did not anticipate was a pop by from the boss. He talked to me for eleven minutes but it seemed like forever as I knew there was a man down I had to help.

I finally brushed the boss and hot-footed it to the can. I rounded the corner just in time to see my buddy come OUT of the bathroom. He instantly saw me and his face morphed into a twisted bewilderment bordering on panic. My Favorite

ME: "What's up, bro?"

BUDDY: "That wasn't you in the stall next to me was it?"

ME: "Obviously not. How could I be out here if I'm in there?"

BUDDY: We gotta get outta here now!

Euphemisms for #2 Time

Hanging a monkey tail
Purging a plumpy
Honking a dirt snake
Dropping a stink pickle
Baking a Back Door Brownie
Cranking a Crispy Coily
Dropping a load of ass raisins
Big, steaming pile of ass nuggets
Choking the Bowl
Firing a Butt Scud
Igniting a Rectal Rocket
Logging On For a Huge Download
Creating a Grunt Sculpture
Pinching a Grumpy
Releasing the Hounds
Serving Up a Fuzzy Butt Burrito
Stocking The Pond With

After ducking into the break room, the story began to emerge into one of the greatest buddy tales of all time and it all started with a mistaken shoe identification.

ME: "You wanna' tell me what the fuck we're running from, man?"

BUDDY: "When I walked in the bathroom, the other stall had somebody in it. When I sat down, I recognized your shoes. Since you weren't saying anything at all, I figured you were just trying to be funny. So I just started talking crazy to get you to laugh. I said my anus was dilated to nine and I may need help delivering this turd baby. Nothing. Complete silence. I just thought you were committed to fucking with me. So I committed to breaking you.

ME: "No way. What the hell did you do?"

BUDDY: "The first thing I did was reach UNDER the stall and pulling toilet paper from his roll. I was certain that would break you. Not a peep. Not a snicker. Nothing. "

ME: "Damn! I can't believe you did that!"

BUDDY: "Yeah, that wasn't even the finale. Since that didn't work, I decided to go next level."

ME: "What the hell was next level, bro?" His face glowed with the red of shame but he gulped and continued.

BUDDY: "Dude, I wiped my ass and then took the paper and showed it under the stall"

ME: "Hold on! You sick son of a bitch. You're telling me that you just showed your doo doo tickets to a complete stranger?"

BUDDY: "Yep. That's why I wanted to get out of there."

We often discussed which employee occupied stall number two. We wondered why they never said a word. Perhaps he was too freaked out. But either way, somewhere in central Arkansas, there's another man telling a story about the worst thing that ever happened to him in a shitter. Sorry bro but, now at least, you are a legend. – PB

Fire: The Original Environmental Sin

Militant environmentalists are happy to offer themselves up on the sacrificial alter of annihilation because they feel it is the only way to cleanse the offense of using fire. Yep: that's where it all began. A gazillion years ago when man first learned to control fire it became our first infraction against nature.

- Fire required wood.
- Wood required disrespecting trees.
- The more fire we needed, the more wood was required. Not enough dead trees? Cut down the live ones.

Then, we realized all that we could do with fire: cook food, scare away animals, heat ourselves, bake pottery, and even melt metals. As we evolved, we consumed more varied resources but, it all began with fire.

Fire is the original sin.

If you had any decency you'd run out right now to the nearest Japanese steakhouse and douse every hibachi with bottled Ethos water to cleanse it of its offense. I know Ethos is holy water because I have it on good word that married bloggers have started to have their newborns baptized by baristas in sinks full of Ethos water at Starbucks.

Most of us consciously or subconsciously try to hide our unclean relationship with fire. Today, the concept of using natural resources to keep warm masquerades as your heating unit and thermostat. Even so, many daring humans still burn wood in fireplaces and wood stoves for heat and comfort, risking condemnation. Fire is at the very source of everything bad with the world, according to the far-left greenies.

And just so it's clear: it's perfectly okay to worry about climate change on a global scale but not climate change in your home. Every time you turn on your air conditioner, another cloud dies. Just remember that.

Without fire we wouldn't have people smoking cigarettes and second-hand smoke would be nonexistent. Without fire, the spark from a spark plug couldn't ignite a gasoline combustion engine and we wouldn't have greenhouse gas emissions. Without fire, no arsonist could ever burn down a California forest again. Without fire, Michael Jackson's hair would have never been burned during that Pepsi commercial, he would have never gone on pain killers, and he'd probably be alive today.

Alright, three out of four is enough. – CD

Prayer to Cleanse Your Fire Sins

Our Mother, which art in the forest,
Hallowed be her name.
Thy Animal Kingdom come,
Thy will be done, protect Earth as it is so holy.
Give us this day, our useful legs
And forgive us our SUVs, as we forgive those who
drill for oil against us.
But, deliver us from Global Warming.
For thine is the Animal Kingdom, and the solar
power, and the glory, for ever and ever.
PETA.

Ever Had a Colonoscopy? Patrick's Preparation Journal

Tomorrow I go in for a colonoscopy so tonight I get the pleasure of becoming substantially lighter. It's like backdoor bulimia!
For those interested in taking the colonoscopy preparation ride with me, I will now begin a journal. I expect it to take until midnight. It may get a little less lucid as I go on as A) I will be drained and B) I can only drink clear liquids and vodka is one so....we shall begin.

- 4:00pm - I have not eaten all day and had to turn off the TV because every effing five seconds McDonalds and Wendy's mocked my very existence. I am happy I know get to ingest something. It is to help me "clean out".
- 4:01pm - I now am about to drink my bottle of poop water. It says Lemony on the front which is encouraging.
- 4:02pm - Lemony is a goddamn lie! It tastes like antifreeze and alka seltzer and goes down like three day old gravy.
- 4:04 pm - God make this bottle empty faster! Why doesn't Stoli's make a poop drink? Can I mix this with vodka? Damn.

- 4:05pm - My stomach has started a rebellion! Where is Muammar Gaddafi when you need him?
- 4:10pm - My stomach literally feels like I am stuck in the moment where the roller coaster drops. It's like there's a miniature donkey inside kicking the shit down my intestine. Life is good.
- 4:13pm - There's NO WAY it can work THAT fast.
- 4:17pm - False alarm but I am pretty sure that I broke the sound barrier with the fart that happened.
- 4:23pm - I feel it now. It appears Hurricane Irene is moving south towards my a**shole.
- 4:24pm - Have opted to put on some loose-fitting elastic shorts. I think jeans MAAAAY be a complication I don't need.
- 4:27pm - Will attempt a cigarette. Very frightened of dragging on it too hard. VERY FRIGHTENED.
- 4:53pm - I began to walk back from the bathroom and Round 2 began. I can see I may have to get my laptop out soon.
- 4:58pm - Sooooo hungry. I would punch my momma for a double stack right now.
- 5:11pm - I know I am supposed to stay hydrated but after the lightening

succession of rounds 3-6 I am beginning to resent my bottle of vitamin water.

- 5:15pm - Round 7 is calling my name. Meanwhile, my a**hole is calling the paramedics.
- 5:30pm - My contractions are now 8-10 minutes apart and my sphincter is dilated to 4.
- 5:35pm - My wife and boys just told me they were going to "run an errand". Asswipes I know you went to eat! TRAITORS!
- 5:41pm - In rap songs when they say, "Make it rain"....I thought it was something else all together. Now I am guessing they are all getting colonoscopies.
- 5:48pm - MUST. HAVE. SMOKE. Glad house surrounded by trees. Will take emergency bucket to deck.
- 6:03 pm - Sometimes being married to a comedian helps and by help I mean the opposite. My wife called and asked if I felt more "pooptastic" or "shitarrific". I laughed and almost shit myself. Thanks honey.
- 6:11pm - In all my fatigue, I failed to realize we passed the 6pm mark. This means I am now NOT an alcoholic if I add Vodka to my clear liquid diet!

- 6:43 pm - almost time for the second bottle of poop water. Just like my priest once told me...this might hurt a little.
- 7:00pm - Bottle # 2 begins.
- 8:34 PM - I know I have been absent a while but I was being held at gunpoint by my a**hole. My youngest heard me in the bathroom and asked if we should call 911. I said yes. Laura stopped him. DAMN SHE DEVIL!
- 8:44 PM - If anyone knows a priest, please send them to my house. I need an exorcism performed on my a**hole!
- 8:46 PM - it's hard to stay hydrated when you're shi**ing and weeping at the same time.
- 8:52 PM - Guys just showed up in hazmat suits and are draping plastic around my bathroom like it's an outbreak. Think E.T. and I don't mean extra turd because there are none.
- 9ish - Dear God. Why do you hate me so. Now I have to take Dulcolax tablets, too?
- 9:18pm - My wife is so good to me! I went to the pantry to get a paper towel and she thought I was going to eat. She didn't want me to ruin all my hard work so she clotheslined me. That's REAL love.
- 9:28 PM - My contractions are now 2 minutes apart and my sphincter is dilated

enough to give birth to the fiery demon that must be in there. Please don't let him be breach!

- 9:35 PM - Dear God. Please let this end. It feels like my a**hole was roundkicked by Chuck Norris while his shoe was on
- 9:40 PM - Governor Beebe just declared my restroom a disaster area and has asked police to set up a one mile perimeter.

Man vs. Time
Calendars - Part 1

Stonehenge

Did you know Stonehenge was a calendar? The Brits built it 4,000 years ago to determine seasonal or celestial occurrences like the summer solstice and lunar eclipses. Most historians agree that Stonehenge was actually designed after observing a typical mouthful of badly maintained English teeth. It was homage to the Druid god known as Dentalostotis.

The real challenge to the Druids was not building Stonehenge. It was carrying the 40 foot toothbrush back and forth to the monument each night in order to clean it. On certain nights of the year, the Druids would gather at the base of Stonehenge and floss between the giant teeth-like columns with large pieces of rope. That's why, even to this day, there is no trace of gum disease anywhere at Stonehenge. Sadly, the same cannot be said about a typical set of British choppers.

Boy, aren't you glad we found a better way to keep track of the year than monolithic pieces of stone? It must have been hell on insurance agents who wanted to send a yearly "gift" to clients.

If you're like me, every year my insurance agent sends me a calendar. It's a great relationship: I give him thousands of dollars-a-year to protect my home and car, and in return he sends me a $2.00 calendar with his company logo splattered across the top. If he really wanted to get my attention he'd fly over to England and get a digital image of "State Farm" plastered across the top of one of Stonehenge's pillars. Now that would be a calendar memento! - CD

Few Know that Stonehenge Was Designed to Look Like a Lower Set of Dentures

Science Is Gonna' Make Your Poop Smell Good

Scientists are using genetics to hack your body. Scientists claim switching up your microbiomes it could make your poop not smell or have a personalized smell. A team led by scientist Gilad Gome is working on manipulating bacteria called lactobacillus that can help you medically, but can also introduce "pleasant scents or flavors" to your vagina.

Are you frickin kidding me!?

I'm completely torn here. On one hand, I just couldn't be more excited about floating a French Vanilla Fart right in the elevator. Some guy will be like, "DUDE! You just dropped an SBD! Silent but Delicious! All the phrases will have to be reinvented. "Whiff it up, bro! I just cut the cheese… danish!"

I can't wait to smell your Christmas ass. "Hey, man. Check this out. Does that not smell JUST LIKE a real wood fireplace? It kinda burns like one, too!"

And I know you guys out there are already dreaming of your girl styling a blueberry brazillian. You're sitting there thinking about it like your girl's nether region was snow cone stand. But you need to stop. All of you. There is a significant danger. Women are vastly more devious than men. This is too much power. Because the first creative ho that turns that thing into a bacon biscuit is gonna' start World War 3. "You like that? You oughtta check out the Starbucks I got brewing next door! Here it comes. Just let that Pumpkin Spice warm you up. Breakfast in bed!"

People, that's not how it's supposed to work. Things on your body smell bad to let you know to stay the hell away. And, the absolute best thing about Heinous Anus is seeing the surprise on your buddy's face when he walks into it. Please don't take that from me. It's just not as funny when you fart French Toast. A real man's gas should smell like Satan's Litterbox not the Hallmark Store. – PB

Man vs. Time
Calendars – Part 2

The Sumerians

The history of calendars is long. 5,000 years ago the Sumerians had a calendar which split the year into 30 months, sectioned off each day into 12 periods (2 hours apiece) and then divided those periods into 30 more little Sumerian minutes. So, each of their "minutes" was about the length of 4 of our current minutes. This would have been good news for some of you guys who are a little "fast on the trigger" in bed. At least if your girlfriend called you a "minute man" you could take solace in the fact that you were actually a "4 minute man" in our thinking.

Of course, our 8-hour workday was more like 2 hours by the Sumerian "clock". The down side: your coffee breaks would be about 3 minutes long and your lunch break about 8 ½ minutes. You would barely have time to play Minesweeper on your abacus let alone surf for any eyefuls of naked women at the secret hole-in-the-wall to their bathroom. - CD

Bad Idea #7,346

A Japanese scientist named Ikeda was asked to research ways to recycle sewer mud. Which is exactly what you think ….poop. He came up with a great idea. You might think fertilizer, maybe some kind of paper product or fabric but nope…. How about burgers?

Ikeda's process begins by extracting protein and lipids from the "mud." The lipids are then combined with a reaction enhancer, then whipped into "meat" in an exploder. He admits that "some people" may have a psychological aversion to eating artificial meat made of their own poop at first but notes that the burgers are extremely low in fat.

Are you frickin kidding me!

A psychological aversion? Your Goddamned right they do! No matter what you do….you can put it through an acid vat, nuclear radiation, particle accelerator. .in the end, it's still a turd. No matter what kind of bun you put it on, ketchup, mustard, Heinz 57….no matter how you dress it. It's still a big ole Shit sandwich! Did we run out of soy and tofu? Matter of fact, even if we have. We'll literally have to run out of EVERYTHING before I consider that. Even Beets.

If I lived in the African desert and hadn't eaten for days and you drove up in your shiny turd burger mobile and offered to feed me. I'd say, "I

think I'll gnaw on this cactus some more. Thanks."
"But sir, you might die." "Yeah but I'll die with
some dignity and no doodoo breath". I could be
one of those starving African kids you see on TV
with the flies all over their eyes and I would eat the
flies before a turd burger. Because. It's. A. DAMN.
TURD!

You can enhance the recipe, add spices and
sauces and whatever the hell you want but I will
guarantee you Mr Ikeda, you will never, ever, ever,
EVER drive through McDonalds and hear,
"Welcome to McDonald's! Would you like to try a
delicious turd burger today." Even the Hamburgler
wouldn't steal that. And if he accidentally did he'd
probably come back and stab you to death. He'll be
the ham-murderer. All because you got him to eat
poop. – PB

Man vs. Time
Calendars – Part 3

The Chinese

Our Chinese friends are not only known for great food you can bring home but a calendar which they perfected around 500 BCE. In case you didn't know, BCE alternately stands for "Before the Common Era", "Before the Christian Era", "Before the Current Era", or "Before Credit Extended" as in buying up U.S. debt in the form of Treasury notes.

The Chinese were working on their calendar forever and the earliest evidence of a Chinese calendar was found on oracle bones of the Shang dynasty. Wow, whose idea was it to create a calendar using some guy's bones - and just how did they find volunteers for that?

Wait a minute - maybe this was the original "Chinese take out" - so to speak. (And I thought it would be a stretch to get my insurance agent to drop a "State Farm" banner from a pillar at Stonehenge!) Can you just imagine soliciting for this job?

One Day at the Ancient Chinese Calendar Shop

Head Calendar Maker: *So, I'm sure all of you oracles are wondering why we asked you to come here today.*

Oracle #1: *Is it about the baloney sandwich that disappeared from the staff refrigerator?*

Head Calendar Maker: *No, no. We have a little project the Shang folks have asked us to complete. Any of you know what a calendar is?*

Oracle #2: *Yeah: it's that thing with holds in the bottom that you drain your spaghetti in.*

Head Calendar Maker: *No. That's a colander. A calendar is something that keeps track of the days of the week.*

Oracle #3: *What's a day?*

Head Calendar Maker: *It's the time between when the sun rises in the morning and the next time it rises.*

Oracle #1: *It is? I thought that was a week! No wonder Christmas keeps coming around so fast!*

Head Calendar Maker: *Alright, look: we have to make a calendar that keeps tracks of the days and years and unfortunately, the only thing we can think of is using some oracle bones.*

Oracle #2: *I vote for finding the guy who took the baloney sandwich. It was a heinous crime and deserves retribution.*

Oracle #3: *I vote for Oracle #1. I mean, he's been celebrating Christmas for Christ's sake! What kind of Chinese oracle does that?*

Head Calendar Maker: *Okay, look. Come back in a week and I'll have a decision.*

Oracle #1: *How will we know when a week has passed? We don't have a calendar yet.*

    - CD

Doctor, I have
An Eel in My Ass!

We all hear those crazy stories from the ER. But this may just take the cake. A man sought emergency treatment because he had an eel stuck up his bottom. It is "unclear" how the eel managed to be trapped inside the man. Medics successfully removed it and the man was later discharged. The article I read goes on to say that the man chose to remain anonymous for this report.

Are you frickin kidding me!

Chose to remain anonymous? They write that like it comes as a surprise. You know what would surprise me? If a dude who went to the ER to get a sea creature extracted from his poop chute opted to actually GIVE his name. "Am I the guy that decided to put an eel where the sun don't shine? Hell yeah. Bob Jones is the name. Eel loving is my game! Pleased as hell to meet ya!"

First of all, no matter what they said at the Eel store, I'd be scared to death it was an electric eel. You turn on some soft music, dim the lights, get your eel ready and then, "Do you smell that? It smells like someone's ass is on fiiiiiir....oh my god!".

Then to walk into the ER and tell em you have a little something-something going on in the ole pooper. Damn bro. What did you tell the doctor? You just flew in from the Bahamas and didn't really notice it until you got off the plane? And if you're the on call surgeon, you're like..."I went to school for 8 years for this?"

But the one I feel the absolute worst for....the eel. What were his last moments like? One minute your swimming and the next everything goes black and stinky. I bet ...at the moment...he wished he were an electric eel.

But, let me sum this up. Bro, if it has come to the point that jamming sea creatures in your keister is the only thing that does it for ya, you might wanna' explore serious therapy or try banging your head against the wall until everything goes black....just like poor Mr Eel. - PB

Man vs. Time
Calendars – Part 4

The Romans

The Romans had a series of early calendars which eventually were really screwed up around 753 B.C. by Romulus, the founder of Rome. In the dysfunctional brain of Romulus, January and February didn't exist and the year started with Martius followed by Aprilis, Maius, Lunius, Quintilis, and Sextilis. The months sounded like judges from a gay fashion show on *Bravo*. Then, all of a sudden after Quintilis came September, October, November, and December.

In Romulus' head, the year only had 304 days and 61 of them occurred in the winter and weren't even designated to any month. Explanation? Well, did I mention Romulus and his brother Remus were nursed by a wolf? It's a long story but I think you can infer from that fact he walked away from the experience with a few issues. Not to mention Romulus smacked his brother over the head with shovel and killed him. I suppose most of his friends thought there was just enough crazy going on in Romulus to let him "lose" 61 days if it made him feel any calmer.

The Julian Calendar was created by Julius Caesar in 46 B.C. This made a little more sense because it had 365 days, 12 months, and even a "leap day" in February once every four years. If he were smart, he would have designated March 15 (the Ides of March) "leap day" to remind him to leap the hell out of the way of that dagger Brutus eventually plunged into his chest. - CD

Man vs. Time
Calendars – Part 5

The Christians

Finally, we get to the Gregorian Calendar. That's the one you ordered from Amazon.com last year which featured the "Cat of the Month". Well, not the cat part but the rest of it. The Gregorian Calendar was signed off on by Pope Gregory XIII in February, 1582. If he had really thought this through he would have captured the "end-of-the-world" glory for the Catholic Church by designating December 22, 2012 as something like "Jesus Sponge Bath Day".

One Day at the Vatican

Pope Gregory XIII: *Let it be known that on December 22, 2012 the world will be consumed by water that will flow from a giant sponge brought back by the second coming of Christ which will hover above the Earth and destroy mankind.*

Nearby Convenient Jew: *Uh, Pope? No can do. The water thing's been done. Remember the rainbow promise?*

Pope Gregory XIII: *But, that was fresh water.*

Nearby Convenient Jew: *And sea water.*

Pope Gregory XIII: *No, I mean, it wasn't soiled. I'm talking about soiled water. It's a metaphor for the sin of all mankind. The Giant Sponge will be brought back by Jesus and he'll park it, say, over Des Moines. Then, through his magnificence, it will be squeezed and all will perish.*

Nearby Convenient Jew: *Sounds really creative but, I don't make the rules.*

Pope Gregory XIII: *Okay. How about the Giant Bucket of Man-Eating Shellfish?*

Nearby Convenient Jew: *You want Jesus to sic giant clams on all human kind?*

Pope Gregory XIII: *Acid-Spewing Dragons Dragging Claws Across a Terribly Oversized Chalkboard?*

Nearby Convenient Jew: *This is sad.*

Pope Gregory XIII: *I'm the freakin' Pope. Don't I get to predict the destruction of anything?*

Nearby Convenient Jews: *Don't you think The Crusades destroyed enough?*

Pope Gregory XIII: *(sighs) Always a bridesmaid, never a bride.*

So, after all this calendar refinement over thousands of years we wind up basing our daily machinations on a calendar by a Pope - yet fear an incomplete calendar created by some dope. Yes, I said dope. Instead of leaving behind a legacy of completeness, some Mayan calendar maker leaves us with an implied prophecy of end times.
Slacker.

As I was writing this, an Associated Press story related the thoughts of a Mayan elder from Guatemala name Apolinario Chile Pixtun. He was pretty "fed up" with all this end-of-the-world stuff and tried to pass it off as stupid Western hysteria as opposed to Mayan ideas.

Well, isn't that just a kick in the pants? I don't know about you, but my life just seems a little incomplete without the dread of a cataclysmic event hanging over my head. Besides, Obama Health Care kicks in 2012.

That's reason enough to feel doomed. - CD

A Short History of Men Grilling

Contrary to popular belief, fire was invented after man began grilling. The first grill was a rock. It was not even a flat rock so meat was always falling off one side into the dirt. For those who do not know, dirt is one of the lousiest seasonings available. Even today, hardly any store carries Seasoning Dirt in the spices aisle. If you want it, you have to try and find it online and even if you do, there are usually not very many choices. There's dirt and if you're lucky, you can find Seasoning Topsoil Dirt. But, that's about it!

Anyway, for many years early man would put meat on a stone and allow the heat of the day to cook his meal. This worked out in some areas but, not all. Putting meat on a stone also allowed mankind to invent another useful tool: the Meat Sundial. As the meat sat on the stone for hours and the sun revolved around it, early man was able to tell what time it was by the shadow the meat cast. It worked great until the meat was cooked. Then, once it was taken off the stone early man was thrown into complete chaos without any way to know if it was lunch time, supper time, or even night time. Yes, without the Meat Sundial, mankind was very confused and light and dark seemed the same. Early man was kind of a dumbass.

But, back to grilling. Eventually, man figured out that a flat stone was superior to a round stone and the sudden usefulness of flat rocks made the price soar from "formerly free for anyone to lift and drag home" to "I will bash your head in if you take it before me." Yes, the first currency was actually flat stones and people killed each other over them. Maybe that's why today we often say "Money is the root of all evil." It apparently started with Neanderthals fighting over a bunch of rocks.

During Roman times, many people enjoyed the activity of grilling their food. Sometimes, Christians were not thrown to the lions for fun but instead, were given the choice of being in charge of keeping the grill going. By this time, Romans were using charcoal weekly and every Saturday night the Emperor insisted on being called the Kingsford. I believe it comes from an old Italian word which means "what a fucking mess" or something like that. Of course, no homage to early grilling could be told without noting Rome's biggest and best griller: Nero. Possibly you heard the story of how Nero fiddled while Rome burned? It all started when he was barbecuing some chicken and a spark flew onto a nearby statue of Vulcan and it caught on fire. Vulcan was the God of Fire and you can imagine his dismay when Nero disrespected him like that. Rome was as good as toast. This really burned Vulcan who decided to torch the whole town. Some of the other Gods thought this was a bit of an overreaction which is why he was later banished to the ends of the Universe by Pansyass, the God of Crybabies.

After Rome burned, grilling stopped for centuries. It just wasn't worth risking a whole city in flames for a lousy hot dog. Then, in 1952, George Stephen, Sr. at Weber Brothers Metal Works in Chicago invented what would become the famous Weber Grill. The Weber grill put safety back into grilling and dared men to douse charcoal with as much lighter fluid as possible – and not burn their houses down. So far, reviews are mixed on that. But, in the meantime, grilling has made a huge comeback worldwide and today millions of men grill beef, chicken, pork, and even fish even more millions of times-a-day.

Except for a handful of Vegans who try and grill tofu and veggie-burgers. The Roman God of Pansyass still watches over those pathetic humans.

- CD

Corey's Meatloaf Burger

During the course of the officially recognized grilling season every year, a certain amount of unfortunate situations present themselves because people either don't listen, don't care, flip off the peace officer, or wind up the ringer in an illegal cop boxing match. Well, listen: there will be plenty of time for horsing around later. I discovered this recipe quite by accident following my born and bred instincts.

2 lbs of ground beef
BacCos
Dried Onions
Italia Bread Crumbs
Ketchup (We put a lot in)
1 Egg

Mix all the ingredients together and when it come to the BacCos, dried onion, and bread crumbs, don't meaure. Just use your discretion.
Let sit for 10 minutes.

Form into patty sized you wish to cook and keep heat on medium-high. Grill to visual delight and remove. You can serve meatloaf burgers with a brown sauce on or without a bun. You can also serve it as a hamburger with ketchup, lettuce, and condiments.

Men and Health – A Pictorial

The Reason You Can No Longer Smoke in Restaurants.

Now this is what men used to like to smoke: "burley" cigarettes that were "toasted!" We're not sure what that really means but to be fair, anything toasted is generally better than the same thing raw. Nobody like raw bread for breakfast – we like it toasted. Few people like raw peanuts – most like them toasted. So, if that makes tobacco better, we're for it. Just don't poach it because that sounds like a sissy move.

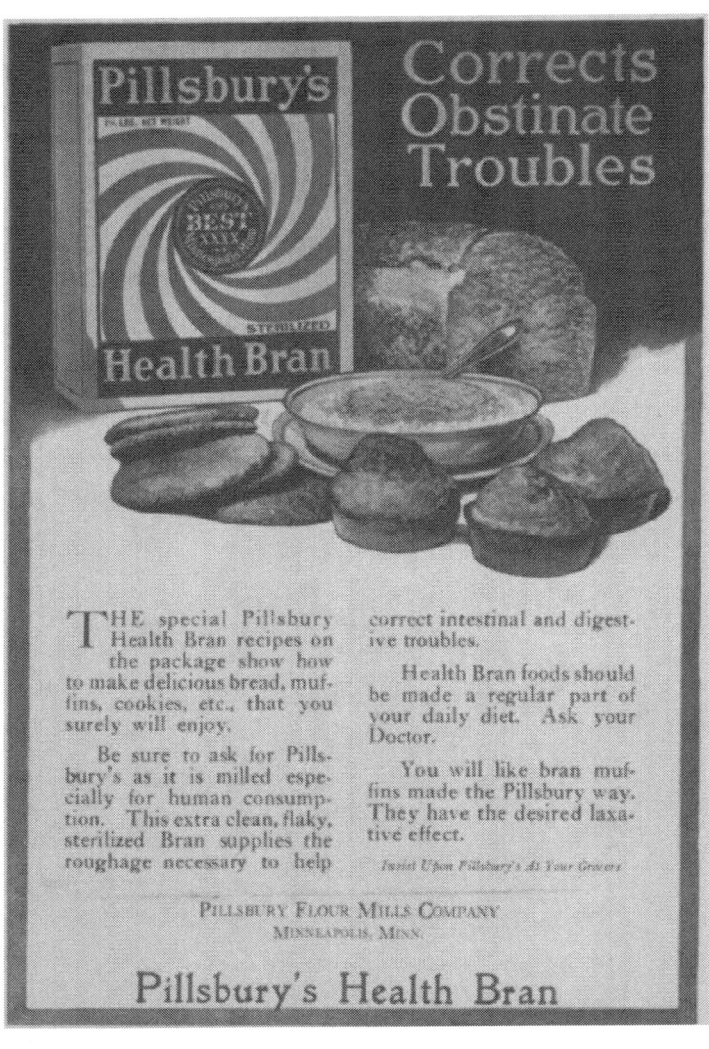

This is why men don't like bran. They don't trust any company that calls "constipation"

"obstinate troubles." Obstinate trouble is your dip-wad brother-in-law who never listens to your perfectly good advice and fucks everything up all the time.

Did you know the Hindenburg Offered First Class accommodations and was a smoking flight?

We don't see this guy holding a muffler. We see a guy getting a prostate exam. How about you?

For coat tails, the telltale's the looking glass!

With us, you see the fit before you order.

Fabrics—the most expensive tailor shows no finer.

Style—advanced or conservative, as you prefer.

Price—about half a fine tailor's.

Dinner Jackets (or Tuxedos) to match.

Hats, shoes and fixings, too.

ROGERS PEET COMPANY

Broadway at 13th St.   "The   Broadway at 34th St.
                        Four
Broadway at Warren Corners" Fifth Ave. at 41st St.

NEW YORK CITY

Men and their asses or:
The very early beginnings of the Bravo Channel.

Corey's Turkey Burgers That Don't Taste Like Shit

In my quest to eat healthier, I have learned to like many turkey versions of other foods. Some aren't so bad, some are taste worse than Donald Trump swallowing his pride. That's why I came up with a recipe to make turkey burgers taste halfway decent. Now, let me explain I don't always use precise amounts of ingredients because real men don't hold measuring cups, okay? So, use this recipe template and decide for yourself what you like more or less of.

1 lb. ground turkey
Shredded cheese
BacOs or some other bacon bit flavoring
Montreal Steak seasoning
Dried onion (as in the condiment & spice kind)
Water

Place turkey into bowl, add cheese, BacOs, and dried onion, and Montreal Seasoning as desired.
Mix thoroughly.
If it seems a little too dry, just add a bit of water.

After it is mixed, make into patties (not too small because that's for little girls) and let it sit for 15 minutes.

Grill as you wish and serve. - CD

The Good, the Bad, and the Moldy

Not all mold is bad. Penicillin was developed from mold, many cheeses taste better because of mold, and without mold you wouldn't have Quorn. I had heard of Quorn before but didn't know what it was until I looked it up. Quorn is actually a brand name for a mycoprotein which is marketed as an alternative to meat. And what is a mycoprotein? In short: protein from fungus. They love Quorn in the UK and Ireland. *God Save the Quorn!* Doesn't it sounds absolutely disgusting?

Wikipedia says, "Quorn is extracted from a fungus, Fusarium venenatum, which is grown in large fermentation vats." Vegetarians love Quorn because it's like eating a cow, only made of fungus. They really do have Quorn burgers, hot dogs, and "products resembling sliced meat."

Here's a clue: anytime you have to use the world "resembling" to describe your product, you've lost me. Yet, the British-based Vegetarian Society has given Quorn its seal of approval. Let's think about this for a second. They like Quorn because it looks like meat but isn't *really* meat. That's like saying you want to have sex with a mannequin in the display window at Macy's because it *looks* female but really *isn't* a female. Listen up you mannequin-banging meatheads (sorry - Quornheads): I'm on to you.

You like the meat, you just can't take the peer pressure from your VegHead friends. Let me ask you: have you ever known someone who "became" a vegetarian just so they could keep getting laid? I know several people who openly admit their relationship is the reason they gave up meat. That's pathetic! What kind of companion holds their lover hostage over a cheeseburger?

There's a famous book on relationships by John Gray entitled, *Men are from Mars, Women are from Venus*. I'd like to update that right now: *Men are from Steak, Women are from Yogurt*. - CD

Man Fears: Zombies

The idea of zombies originated in the Afro-Caribbean belief system of Voodoo which "... told of the people being controlled as laborers by a powerful sorcerer." The perfect zombie comes back to life after death without speech or free will. I know what you're thinking: sounds like a perfect spouse, right?

In the 1980s, a Harvard ethnobotanist named Wade Davis proposed a pharmacological case for zombies through two book he wrote: *The Serpent and the Rainbow* (1985) and *Passage of Darkness: The Ethnobiology of the Haitian Zombie* (1988). Davis concluded a person could be turned into a zombie by introducing two powders into the blood stream: tetrodotoxin (the poison from puffer fish) and datura. These two ingredients allegedly produce a death-like state where the victim is susceptible to direction.

So, theoretically, a person can become a zombie or at least think he's one. A zombie attack is not just science fiction.

To illustrate my point, witness the zombie incident that occurred in Iowa City, Iowa on October 25, 2009. According to police, a man accused another man of being a zombie. Then, he punched him twice.

LaCrosseTribune.com reported: "A man was ordering food when he was approached by another man who called him a zombie, then hit him in the eye. When the victim tried to call police on his cell phone, the man punched him again, breaking his nose. The man then ran out a back door."

With zombies, you have to be proactive. If you want to survive a zombie attack you're going to need the right weapons: a shotgun, plenty of shells, a shovel, and one of my inventions: a pork chop in the shape of Glenn Beck's head. Always aim for the head with the shotgun and when you run out of bullets, decapitate them with your shovel. Wear the Beck- shaped pork chop to help ward them off because most zombies are reanimated corpses of mindless human beings - you know: Democrats. You don't believe me? Look how many dead people voted in the last Chicago election. (Or is that most Democrats are zombies?) Either way - trust me on this - the pork chop will fend them off. - CD

NOTICE

Zombies: my neighbor is tastier. Two houses down on left.

TXT2PIC.COM

Spontaneous Vocabulary

These are words and phrases Corey & Patrick have made up on-the-air, on-the-fly

Buffing the Cow - Masturbation

Brain Buffering – When your brain can't handle the failure of the internet to connect.

Junksgiving – The real purpose of the superbowl, i.e. junk food.

'Nier – The opposite of "Truther." A 'Nier denies all.

Man Décor – The term for an ornamental testicle and/or medical replacement testicle

Bonus Hole – Any orifice in the human body which can be used for a second, sexual purpose other than its original intention.

Equivilate - Equal to

Coming Out of the OR – Declaring one a transgender, as in "Coming out of the Closet" but, in this case you came out of an operating room.

Trans-Action – Getting it on with a any kind of "Trans" (as in transgender, transvestite, trans-sexual)

Trans-Former – A transsexual who is post-operation

Eighty-ist – One who hates on all who don't think the 1980s define the world.

Spliff Personality – One whose personality is largely defined by the weed they smoke.

Stuck on the Couch – High as hell.

Bringin' the Brisket – When you are kickin' serious ass

Peoplepedia – When various people tell differing versions of the truth

Short End of the Foam Finger – A raw deal, possibly stinky and scandalous

Media Echo – When you hear the same thing you just heard on the radio or TV seconds after it was said

Twee-Gret – A tweet that you regret sending

Dream Drool – Actual drool or evidence of dried drool still on your face after you wake up.

Taint You Off The Air – talking about dirty things
NOT suitable for the audience – CB & PB

The Food Police
Are On My Tail

We have a strange relationship with food that is unlike anything else in life, except maybe marijuana, but that could explain, well, never mind. We plan a lot of life around food. We choose somewhere to eat like picking a football team. You are either Team McDonalds or a member of the Burger King's Royal Family. Not both. You rep your food style like a verbal jersey. I'm a vegan. I eat organic. We. Are. Obssessed (self-included).

We seem to have a particular fascination with the delicious, crispy mouthgasm that you know as bacon. It should be Bacon. It's worthy enough. Yet, sometimes our lust for the pig stick leads us to idiotville.

The makers of a new product insist you need protection in that sensitive area. Behold, the Naked Bacon Cooking Armor. The product, developed by J&D's Foods, is "constructed from a hard plastic shell covered with foam then enclosed in vinyl. It truly is the gold standard of genital grease burn protection." Co-founder Justin Esch, said he hopes the groin protector will also inspire those who do their sizzling with clothes on to take them off. "We're just opening the door.. "With any luck you step through it because happiness is waiting on the other side."

Are you frickin kidding me!?

Happiness? So, as long as the hot ass grease gets me somewhere OTHER than my man stick, no worries? You and I both know that's nuttier than a squirrel's first dump of the day.

What waits on the other side of that door is PAIN. On the pain scale of burns, there's fire, then napalm and then somewhere between flamethrower and the acid blood in that movie Aliens, you will find hot bacon grease. And, aside from the whole POP – OH GOD MY NIPPLE'S ON FIRE grease pop…in all honesty, ain't nobody wants to eat food your naked ass is cooking. Yeah, Bubba. Whip me up one of them BLTs and sprinkle a little pit hair on it for me. And you're like, NUH UH…MY BODY IS SHAVED. First….unless you're an olympic swimmer…that's weird. Second, big deal. All you've done is change seasonings from body hair to dead skin flakes. Ah hellll yeah. That'll make my grilled cheese better. Can we be honest here.

If you are cooking bacon naked, it's probably because there aren't any clothes left that fit your lard ass. STEP AWAY FROM THE BACON FATTY…and head to the Big Un Store and get you some new overalls so you can be buried with dignity following your inevitable heart attack.
– PB

One Day at God's Desk

Angel: *Oh God? We have to assign a few more characteristics to diseases.*

God: *Okay. What do you have?*

Angel: *Parkinson's Disease.*

God: *Make everyone shake. But start it slow then speed it up until they can make good cocktails without a blender.*

Angel: Cancer.

God: *Mmm.... Cancer. Nobody likes Cancer. I know! Give the world something they all want: to lose 50 pounds! Write that down: cancer brings on weight loss. Not a perfect weight loss plan but you should never look a gift horse in the face.*

Angel: *What about Diabetes?*

God: *Diabetics...let's see: Type I, Type II. It's all about the sugar and their eating habits. I think I want to slap a few pounds of fat right smack on those little barrel chested monkeys to remind them that the pen is mightier than the fork.*

Angel: *I thought the expression was The Pen is Mightier than the Sword.*

God: *It is but if you give them a sword they're only going to use it to cut more roast beef.* - CD

The Church of Bacon

Couples headed to Las Vegas to get married are excited about a new option. Hundreds of madly in love meat fans are getting married in a 'church of bacon'. Prophets who spread the word of the 'bacon God' claim to have over 4,000 members. Members can get their own 'bacon wedding' for free and their website also advertises funerals and baptisms. Isn't that romantic?

Are you frickin kidding me!?

That's right. If you can take a break between buffets, roll your lard ass over here and get hitched to your grazing partner. Along with the marriage, we also offer a free pair of stints for your soon to be clogged arteries and, did we mention we also offer funerals? Because, let's face it, that ain't sweat coming out of you. That's 100% uncut grease. Matter of fact, I'm willing to bet that if you one of you caught fire it would smell like Denny's at 5 am. And if that fire sadly resulted in death, there's no doubt that, by the time the coroner arrived, the other would be sitting there with a bib, fork and a ramekin full of honey mustard. (Mouth full) WHAT? I LOVED HIM.

Matter of fact, I'm not certain I didn't just describe the Church of Bacon basic funeral plan.; "Hey, you guys all know Tony ate the finest meats his entire life, now come see just how delicious he is! We've had Tony resting in our signature Church of Bacon smoker for 72 hours and we have plenty of dipping sauces to choose from. We all know this is what Tony would have wanted. Now, let's get this funeral started. Widow fatass, why don't we start with you. Here, try some of your mouthwatering Smoked Husband. The rest of you have a flag at your table, we'll keep bringing Tony around until you put the flag down! Now, let us pray!" - PB

I'm a Food Separatist

I'm worried if my wife and I ever have to go into a survival bunker to avoid the rampaging zombies, we aren't going to see eye-to-eye on the menu. I've come to the realization that we are complete opposites in how we eat our food.

She's a "Mixer and a Masher." She drops and dumps all her food into a bowl like some nutritional backhoe filling in a ditch. It matters not if the meatloaf touches the peas or the creamed carrots crash into the mashed potatoes. The woman has no respect for the individual *dish rights* which all foods are entitled to. Her disregard in this matter actually verges on a form of abuse. More than once I've heard a vegetable cry out, *"Have you no sense of decency? Will no one come to our aid?"*

I will. I am here to free the food.

I'm am a "Food Separatist". I hate my food touching when it's been placed on the same plate. If I could, I'd put up little fences around each particular portion and guard those fences using a cadre of tiny little border patrols. If any pork chop or spoonful of macaroni and cheese even tried to slip past my security guards, it would immediately be detained and lead back to where it belonged. How appropriate it would be - especially when eating tacos and refried beans.

If the federal government won't do it, I will just have to. - CD

Is that a Dildo in Your Happy Meal?

A burger joint in Copenhagen, Denmark is taking fast food down a somewhat darker path. It's now selling sex toys along with hamburgers. Hot Buns is adding dildos, vibrators, whips and other sex-oriented products to the menu. Hot Buns owner Mathias Kaer says the sex toys will only be available in evening hours. He believes he's onto something. He says, "On Friday and Saturday nights there are only two things most people want: sex and food. We're combining them both,"

Are you fricking kidding me!

I'm gonna' pull up and hear,

"Welcome to Hot Buns. Would you like to try our new Bacon & Butts Combo?"

"What's in that?"

"That's a bacon burger, fries and a regular size buttplug. "

"Oh that sounds great! But can we Biggie Size that plug?"

First of all, this is idiotic because who the hell wants burgers and sex? It's one or the other. If you eat burgers and fries you know damn well, even if you wanted to have sex, your bloated stomach says pump the brakes captain happy.

Second, do you how cluttered the menu board is now? It's enough pressure just to find the hamburger I want in that amount of time but now, on top of that, I have to add the excruciating choice between the Manaconda or The R2 Dildo?

How can I, in the span of a few scant seconds truly evaluate the Hot Buns Heavy Duty Hogtie Kit? Are those spring-loaded clips? Are the cuffs soft? And how embarrassing is dine in? Sitting by youself eating the Desperation Burger with your Katy Pervy Love Doll on the table. The gimp at the next table is laughing at you. And don't even get me started on the restrooms. Some dude walks in with a strap on saying, Dude, look what I got in my Strappy Meal! Man, I'm trying to pee here. - PB

A Short History of
the Pep Boys

The Pep Boys started in Philadelphia in 1921 when four Navy buddies - Emanuel "Manny" Rosenfeld, Maurice "Moe" Strauss, Moe Radavitz and Graham "Jack" Jackson - put up $200 apiece to establish an auto parts company. That's right: there were originally two "Moes" but the Radavitz "Moe" left after a few years.

So, you would assume the cartoon caricatures of "Manny, Moe & Jack" were based on the three remaining owners. Not exactly. According to pepboys.com:

"Ironically, the three faces that have become so recognizable around the world as Manny, Moe and Jack, are not truly Manny, Moe and Jack. Jack's face appeared briefly when the caricatures were first penned. However, after Mr. Jackson left Pep Boys, his face was replaced with that of Moe's brother, Isaac (Izzy) Strauss.

After Izzy left the company, Manny Rosenfeld's brother, Murray, joined the team. However, Izzy's face remained and continues to be a part of the company's icon to this day."

I find it disconcerting that The Pep Boys are not who they appear to be. This is almost as bad as when I found out that Chastity Bono wanted an Adam's apple. *The 3 Stooges* had a myriad of personnel changes over their career but at least they never tried to pass off Curly as Shemp.

I didn't realize what a cult following the Pep Boys had until I began to scour around eBay to see what Pep Boy memorabilia people were buying and selling. What I found were Pep Boys bobble head dolls, Pep Boys matchbooks, Pep Boys "Pure as Gold" motor oil, Pep Boys lighter fluid, Pep Boys truck banks, and the rarely acquired Pep Boys "Handy Bulb Kit."

I got so caught up in the fever, I bid on a used Pep Boys gift card (below) which I think captures the boys in their absolute prime. - CD

Whiny Food Bitches

Some are bending to the pressure of a politically correct world of healthy eaters who can't let us fat-asses eat in peace.

Ronald McDonald has gotten a makeover. The fast-food mascot has tamed his wild hair. He swapped his mustard yellow jumpsuit for a stylish red blazer and ketchup-colored bow tie. He now also rocks an updated red-and-white rugby shirt, slimmer yellow pants and a matching vest. That sounds like a great marketing move!

Are you frickin kidding me!

Come on, McDonalds. You're giving in to all these whiny food bitches who want to turn you into a salad shop. Find your McSpine and tell these fools to McSuck it! What you should be doing is going the opposite direction. Yeah, Ronald McDonald should wear a suit. A suit made of 100% all beef patties and his catchphrase should be, "Am I healthy now, bitches?" And yeah, he should wear a tie...made of chicken nuggets. From time to time he should dip it in a pocket full of ranch and just start gnawing on it. And he should wear a chain with a giant clock like Flav-A-Flav with the countdown to triple bypass.

What's next? You gonna' make Grimace lose weight eating wraps? Hell no. You better keep shoveling fries in his fat, purple mouth. Is the Hamburgler gonna' go straight? NO! You load his ass up with weapons. Give him an automatic weapon with a clip full of bacon bits and tell him to grease anyone from PETA who gets within shooting range! 30 pcs of Bacon per second, whore. Now get your kale eating ass back. DUH DUH DUH DUH DUH – You're suckin it!

Your next commercial should be these guys coming out like the Expendables laying down a suppressing fire of McGriddles. They should have the Chihuahua, The King and that dumbass cooking mitt that talks in a P.O.W. camp. That ginger, Wendy, might be worth trying to convert. Hey girl….you like special sauce, right? That's the Ronald McDonald we want. Kids should fear him, women love him and men wanna' be him. Tell me I'm wrong?

You know what we want? We want fast food to be fast and right. That simple. In our sick, codependent relationship with food, we quickly go Jeckyl and Hyde on a sub-par drive-thru employee. – PB

When Kirstie Alley Orders Take Out

Man Pisses Away Earth
Global Warming:
The Snow Cone Scenario

For argument's sake let's say the world is going to end in 2050 and maybe it will start at the North or South Pole. Think of the Polar Ice Caps as huge snow cones. What happens when you start sucking on a cherry snow cone? All the good stuff seems to rise to the surface - the flavor - until the only thing left is bare ice and a hole in the top of the ice from your mouth chomping at or sucking up the small pieces of ice.

Now, magnify that a bazillion times and although it's a simple analogy, you have the destruction of the Polar Ice Caps. Global Warming will suck on the Earth's snow cones and when the flavor is all gone all that will be left is a lot of melted, disturbed ice particles that want only to slip into the sea and become one with the ocean.

As the North Pole melts, thousands of polar bears will be cast into the ocean and set adrift on little ice chunks which will eventually find their way to the lower land masses. When the ice chunks are close to places like London or New York City the polar bears will jump off and rampage through city streets shredding passers-by into mouthfuls of nutrition. And some of you wanted to save these bastards? They will eat you for dinner, starting with the environmentalists who they will conveniently sniff out first. It's just a gift they have.

As evidence, I remind you of the polar bear attack at the Berlin Zoo in April, 2009. Some trusting woman hopped a fence and entered the polar bear living area. She was bitten several times and lucky to be saved by some quick-thinking zoo workers.

In 2006, a man in the Yukon was minding his own business and sleeping in his tent when a Polar Bear tried to eat him. The man survived the bear, barely, and shot it.

Don't let those ads with Polar Bears drinking Coca-Cola fool you: the only "six-pack" these bears are interested in is the one made of muscles sitting on your chest. - CD

The Only Safe Polar Bear is One Made out of Cardboard

Fast Food Felons

Shaneka Torres from Michigan is going to prison after unloading her gun at a Grand Rapids McDonald's after restaurant workers messed up her order, not once but twice. Jurors convicted her in just an hour for the shooting.

What happened? She got a bacon double cheeseburger. It didn't have bacon. Then McDonald's promised to make it up to her with a free sandwich on her next trip. When the SECOND one came without bacon she started shooting but didn't hit anyone. Glad to get this menace off the street!

ARE YOU FRICKIN KIDDING ME!?

Was this a jury of Vegans and PETA members? Who in their right mind would send this woman to prison? She should be appointed as a parenting coach because I GUARANTEE you this lady's kids aren't crying about somebody leaving One Direction. She let em get away with missing the bacon ONCE and didn't even make an example of anyone. And the second time, all she did was fire a couple rounds in the drive thru window? For God's sake, that's a constitutional right. Patrick Henry said, AND I QUOTE.....Give me bacon or give me death! That's why that Nick Cage movie National Treasure is a joke. The Freemasons weren't guarding precious artifacts and gold. They were guarding some Petit Jean Thick Cut Bacon and that Book of Secrets...that's real... only it doesn't have locations of hidden treasure. It has grill recipes that all feature bacon.

And now America owes Shaneka a debt of gratitude. Because I bet you can hit that Micky D's drive through and not a single damn employee will leave the bacon off again. Shaneka you made a difference in the world and one day you will be mentioned alongside the Thomas Jeffersons and John Quincy Adams and regarded as a patriot. – PB

The Green Police

The fact of the matter is: you can never be "green" enough no matter how hard you try. I feel like I'm stuck in some kind of environmental Rubik's Cube and no matter which way it turns and no matter how many plastic water bottles I recycle, I'm still not good enough. Actually, I wouldn't have any plastic water bottles at all if the environmentalists hadn't lobbed the first volley of fear.

It all started when they scared me into drinking bottled water because they said the fluoride in the water supply was bad for me, not to mention the laundry list of medications which wash through our bodies and settle into the reservoirs.

So, we all run out to our supermarkets and buy bottled water. Except for you stuck up loons who are too good for any bottled water. You have to have FIJI bottled water because "...it comes from an artesian aquifer, located at the very edge of a primitive rainforest, hundreds of miles away from the nearest continent."

Visiting the FIJI water website is like finding yourself in San Francisco's Haight-Ashbery district circa 1967. New age music plays, swirls of animated flash-induced waves emanate from a glorious bottle of FIJI and the website discretely links to fijigreen.com where the company explains the status of their carbon footprint, the crusade to become carbon negative, and other talking points which appear to be written by escaped mental patients.

It's *WATER* people!

Wait: you don't know the half of it. FIJI is apparently so important to some people the company will actually sell it to you directly. God knows you can't risk running out of FIJI water! What would you brush your teeth with? That's why you can order an annual subscription - one case a month of 24 bottles - for only $360 dollars-a-year.

Let's put this in perspective. At monthclubstore.com:

The "Jelly of the Month Club" is $176.99

The "Pickle of the Month Club" is $196.99

The "Olive of the Month Club" is $196.99

The "Pickled Veggie of the Month Club" is $196.99

The "Bloody Mary of the Month Club" is $196.99.

And The "Beef Jerky of the Month Club is $276.99

All I know is if I'm' going to pay $360 dollars-a-year for a case of 24 bottles of water to be delivered to my house each month then the UPS guy better be ready to perform *Riverdance* from and *back* to the truck as he's dropping off the package. Plus: that water better cleanse my body better than a high-priced colonic from a cross-eyed Asian lady. – CD

Pizza Continues to be Abused – and we do Nothing!

In case you thought we stopped caring about all the crazy foods at major league ballparks across America—we're actually just scratching the surface. Because now we're moving to the minor leagues and their major flavor like the Triple-A affiliate of the Houston Astros—the Fresno Grizzlies—who have revolutionized pizza as we know it. That's because, this week, fans will be able to feast upon something called the Frankenslice as part of the team's "Halfway II Halloween" promotion. So what is the Frankenslice? Simply put, it's a pizza with hot dogs crammed into its crust.

Are you frickin' kidding me!

Halfway to Halloween? You'll be lucky to make it halfway to the ER. Wooooah ohhhhh we're halfway thereeeee…oh oh total heart failure…That's why they call it Frankenslice cuz you are gonna' be rocking gnarly stitches when they're done with the Franken Bypass. That's the way to get back at the healthcare industry! That's basically like calling Jake from State Farm at three in the morning and asking him if they cover wrecks because you just wrecked his mom.

Where do you go after the frankenslice promotion? How about the chee-dog-chick-slice-steak-bacon ranch rocket? That's where you take a cheeseburger, hotdog, chicken tenders, pizza and steak….tie it to a live pig, smother it in ranch and fire it into the winners mouth using an giant acme slingshot? Ah damn, I forgot the fries. I can't have a chee-dog-chick-slice-steak-bacon ranch rocket without fries. Just so you know, in the affordable healthcare act on page 497, it does state that no insurance company is required to cover a chee-dog-chick-slice-steak-bacon ranch rocket ….but you don't care do ya? – PB

The Man Who Tattooed a Radio Station Logo to His Forehead

This is probably old news to anyone who lives in Davenport, Iowa but probably not to you. This is the story of David Jonathan Winkelman, the man who tattooed his forehead with a radio station's logo.

The story of his forehead tattoo popped up a decade after it was originally ingrained on him because Winkleman was arrested on a misdemeanor and was processed by the law - including a mug shot.

The Smoking Gun website jumped on the story because Winkelman's forehead prominently displays a tattoo featuring a now defunct rock station from Davenport. According to The Smoking Gun:

"Winkelman became a human billboard for the radio station KORB in late-2000 after a disc jockey offered listeners a six-figure payout if they tattooed the FM station's call letters and logo on their forehead. Winkelman and his stepson, Richard Goddard, went to a local tattoo parlor and each emerged with forehead ink promoting '93 Rock,' the 'Quad City Rocker.'"

When Winkleman tried to cash in his deed, the deejay defended it as a joke and station management refused to make good on the offer. Winkleman sued but the case was later dismissed. As do most things in radio, 93 Rock eventually changed format and vanished from the landscape, leaving in its wake KQCS, Star 93.5.

It seems one of the few people who remember 93 Rock is Winkleman, who is reminded of its former glory every time he looks in the mirror.

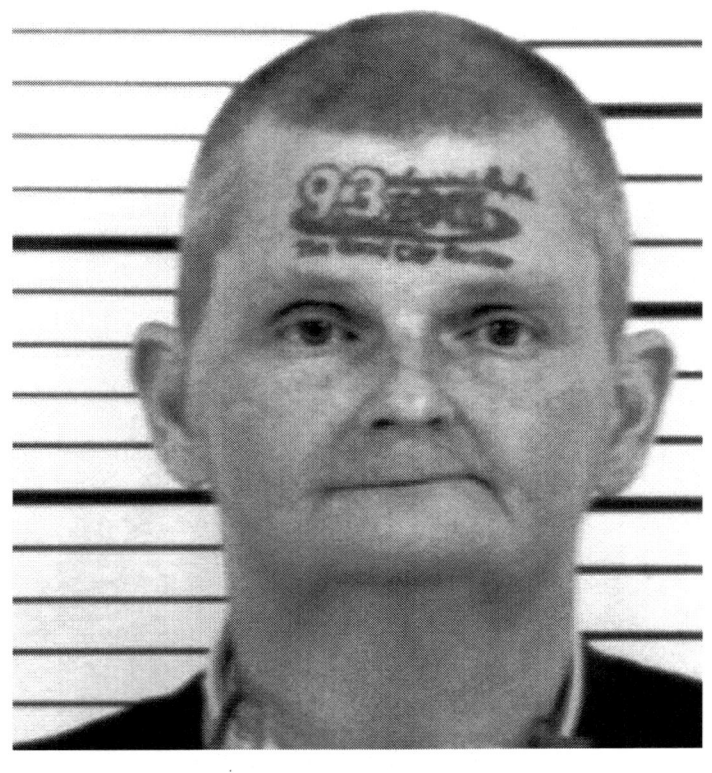

Continuing Budget Cuts Have Limited Radio Advertising to Affordable Venues

Who Put the Doom in the
Doom-De-Doom-De-Doom?

Ever wonder why do so many religions have prophecies of doom?

Wouldn't it be nice if just once a religion came along that predicted something else besides worldwide destruction and disaster? I'd like a religion that predicts everyone gets a coconut cream pie once every 6 days until the "7 Years of Cake" arrive.

Upon the beginning of the "Cake Days" frosting will fall from the skies like manna and angels will produce a magical and endless 6-layer, double-fudge chocolate cake which will feed the world. No more hunger, just high cholesterol.

I will name my religion "Cakism" and the followers Cakatholics.

Communion will feature Hostess frosted cupcakes. Instead of *The Last Supper*, we'll revere *The First Breakfast with Cheese Danish*. Preachers will convene their flock on Sundays, hold up a portrait of Marie Antoinette and remind them:

"Let Them Eat Cake. Amen"

People will drive cars with religious icons on their bumpers that look like a cake knife because the Messiah will be a baker, not a carpenter. During the "7 Years of Cake" no one will gain even a single ounce of fat no matter how much cake they stuff in their pie hole.

Jenny Craig will be banished from the face of the Earth and according to "The Cake Prophecies" it will be written that Kirstie Alley and Valerie Bertinelli will wrestle in Nestles chocolate syrup until a victor is decided. The loser will then be sacrificed to *Cakelis*, the cake god (pronounced káy-ko-lis), by being baked alive inside a lemon meringue pie the size of a Ford 250 pickup truck.

For the record, I considered naming the cake god using an appropriate Latin word until I made a grisly discovery. When I typed into Google "What is the Latin word for cake?" I wound up on a page which said, "...the **placenta** is not exactly what its Latin name implies. The word placenta means *flat cake*. For the Romans it referred to any rounded loaf of cake or bread."

There's no way "placenta" gets to have anything to do with my high calorie religion. Although, it did inspire a thought:

One Day in a Home Where People Pray to Cakelis:

Little Johnny: *Mommy? Where do babies come from?*

***Mommy:** Well, Mommies and Daddies who love each other kiss and make a "baby batter". Then, they cook the batter for 9 months. If the baby is a boy, he lives in a cake. If the baby is a girl, she lives in a loaf of bread. Finally, when the baby is ready, he or she pushes his way out into the world.*

***Little Johnny:** Oh. Maybe that's why one of the kids on the playground said his Mommy had a bun in the oven?*

Alas, Cakism is only a fantasy and nobody has yet to create such a religion. All we have now are religions that promise if you're not good, you're going to hate it when you die. And even if you are good, you're still going to die and then be judged. So, if God is cranky the day you check out, you still might wind up peeling potatoes in Hell's Kitchen for eternity.

No matter what: you're not getting out alive and if you're lucky enough to live until the end-of-the-world you're not only going to die but it's going to be pretty nasty because God is a Drama Queen.

Personally, I like my religion where you get pies and cake. - CD

You are *Already* in the Future!

Technology is amazing. The innovations and inventions of the past decade alone are mind-boggling. Consider your smartphone. How long have you had one? Chances are it hasn't been that long and, yet, can you imagine being without it? At the time I am writing this there are two different medications they are in final testing that will almost stop breast and lung cancer. Drones are flying all over the country taking videos and causing chaos as we try to figure out how the hell to manage drones and the First Amendment.

But, for every amazing innovation there are ten things that should have never seen a green light. Consider this.

Girlplay is a condom company mainly aimed at bold and daring women, changing the whole experience of love-making. It produces a line of spray-on condoms that uses the latest technology to fit each and every size. These spray-on condoms are made for the perfect fit, and function. The idea of the spray on condom extends a conventional condom's life span, increases convenience, and changes the very action of putting on a condom. Photos show shows the condom emanating from an aerosol spray can, like a spray-on bandage.

Are you frickin kidding me!

Airbrushing on a condom? BEST INVENTION EVER! Oh, you wanna' get it on girl? I'll be back in a half hour! Why a half hour? Cuz I'm gonna' build myself a miniature spray booth just like they have at the body shop and I'm gonna' change it up all the time! Get me some little stencils so I can hot rod my junk up with a nice flame package. Tiny little letters that say Super Sport. Oooooh...oooh...maybe I wanna' make it look like a rocket? They should include a tiny astronaut action figure. This is Captain Winky and I'm ready for take off. You just don't wanna' go all Challenger and blow the o-ring. Too soon?

I could paint it to look like a Navy Submarine. Semen reporting for duty, sir! The fun would never end! I could airbrush it to look like ice cream and then ask my unsuspecting wife if she wants a Nutty Buddy! You're in luck, because today I'm your ice cream man...stop me when I'm passing by....Ooooh oooh.....I could make it a Super Soaker. Is that wrong?

Come on people, a spray on condom? Every time you log on Facebook you have to see some idiot who painted his like a 2X4 and is calling himself Hacksaw Jim Dugan. Tommy Lee has his painted like a pogo stick. Actual size. We get it already, Tommy. Porn stars will have their sponsor logos on it like race cars. Does that say?.....yep, Dicks Sporting Goods. – PB

Food of the Gods: Chick-O-Stick

Actually, did you know that Chick-O-Stick has been around since *The Great Depression*? It's true. It's made of peanut butter, sugar, corn syrup, coconut, and coloring. The original candy had a wrapper that featured a chicken wearing a cowboy hat. Probably because the maker, Arkinson Candy Company, is located in Lufkin, Texas.

I suppose if they had been located in Florida, the logo might have featured a chicken sitting in a wheelchair with an IV full of corn syrup. But, trust me: no one wants to buy a food product that features anyone or anything sitting in a wheelchair.

Unless it is Rolled oats.

Chick-O-Stick or Broken Nuclear Uranium Rod from Fukushima? You Decide.

Of course, the success of Chick-O-Stick came after several rather preliminary and highly embarrassing failures by the company which were not generally accepted by the public: Lamb-O-Stick, Oxen-O-Stick, Frog-O-Stick, and the One-Celled-Amoeba-O-Stick with Fruit-Flavored Nucleus. - CD

Get Your Odor Motor Running

This clothing tech just made my brain hurt. There are now jeans on the market – called *Shreddies* – that, supposedly, filter your farts. These high tech pants use an activated carbon lining made from "Zortex," which absorbs and neutralizes all suspicious odors. The company manufacturing this miracle product claims its pants can filter odors 200 times stronger than the average "emission."

Are you frickin kidding me!

Why the hell would anyone buy these? 99% of hole flappers released don't even have odor and who wants to hide the 1% that do? Normal people don't wanna' hide those farts.

When you can bring tears to someone's eye simply by airbrushing your boxers, that's a moment of pride. There's nothing more fulfilling than watching the office tardsicle unsuspectingly walk right into that paint peeling rump ripping flamethrower. But that should only happen like once in a while.

If you're the kind of person who's blowing out the O ring so much you actually would consider buying fart choking jeans....you don't need jeans. You need medical help.

Step one: Whatever you're eating. STOP. And I know the bodybuilders say, "man it's my protein powder". Well, guess what, tough guy? You can beat my ass but I'm still gonna' take your girl. Know why? It doesn't matter how much you look like Magic Mike if your ass is a constant dumpster fire.

And, in all honesty, these things are unproven, new technology. These things may not even be safe. What if those things get too full like the containment unit in Ghostbusters? That means every fart you had trapped in there could come out all at once thus creating the risk of your toxic turd tremors inflicting mass casualties. And, this day and age, you're just one good fart away from me suing you for pain and suffering. – PB

The Moment Corey was Diagnosed with Depression

Doctor: Corey, it is my professional opinion that you are clinically depressed.

Corey: You're right: the prices at your clinic are depressing me.

Doctor: Clinical Depression is a mental disease.

Corey: Wait a minute. Don't tell me that. That's depressing. Is this your idea of a joke? Tell the depressed guy he's mental, too?

Doctor: We have procedures that can help you.

Corey: You mean like hooking an electrode to my head and shocking me?

Doctor: Our shock therapy is 'greener' now. The electrodes are solar powered.

Corey: What happens on rainy days?.

Doctor: There's a 30% chance of you teetering on the edge of normalcy with a high of 78.

Corey: Gee, that sounds like a fair exchange for my mental state.

Doctor: There's new medicine.

Corey: If it doesn't taste like pizza, I can't swallow it.

Doctor: We also still have the lobotomy option available, too.

Corey: I think I like the idea of a lobotomy. Sure, it may turn me into a drooling bucket head but at least it won't preclude me from one day holding public office! - CD

Meysken's Drunk as Shit Chili

Stuff to grab:
1 big brisket
2 big ass jalapeños
1 onion
Bacon don't forget bacon
1 lb ground beef (no turkey, turkeys for girls)
6pk or more of beer any beer
Salt and pepper
Chili powder
Cayan pepper
Spice rum stronger the better
2 cans Rotel
Soak brisket in rum over night (do a shot of remainder of rum)
Next morning fire up the grill and drink a beer.
Smoke the brisket longer the bettner.
Drink a couple of beers while check the brisket (do a shot of remaining rum)

In a big pot cut and cook the bacon, add ground beef cook till done. Drain the grease. Add spices, rotel, jalapeños and 2 beers. Shred the brisket and cook 2 hours low heat. Finish the rum. Ask wife to get cha another beer and fix your plate because your drunk as shi#$. – David Meyskens, Semper Fi Movers

The Edible Mist Machine

Technology even has you vaping your food. Now you can inhale all of your guilty pleasures without giant calories. A company named Lick Me I'm Delicious, says its Edible Mist Machine can emit 200 different "delicious" flavored vapors for your enjoyment. Flavors like lobster, bacon and popcorn. The CEO stated, "The range of flavors is massive and we can also produce you a personalized mist from pretty much anything in the world, like your favorite book or even your hair," he said. "AND it's zero calories." The Edible Mist Machine's "ultrasonic vaporization" makes a mist that basically gives you a hit of flavor without actually ingesting any food.

Are you frickin kidding me!

I can see the testimonials pouring in! "Thanks for making Anorexia so much easier!" "Bulemics rejoice! I don't have to toss my cookies anymore because now I inhale them!" Basically, it's vaping. Vaping bacon. Let me tell you something, if you are into bacon so much you need to vape it, there's a solid chance when you die that they'll have to cut your trailer open like a sardine can to get your lardass down to the crematorium. Plus side....you probably will smell good when they ignite it. Because if you're vaping bacon, that's just a makeshift til you get to the real thing. And you can't go telling people you can make any custom

flavor. Do you know how many sickos are out there? Now some poor lab flunky is gonna' have to make a vape called Goat Love. Do you really want that on your conscience? Special message to the Olson Twins: Please listen to me. It WILL taste like bacon. It is not bacon. It has no food in it. When your stomach starts hurting, that's not a side effect of your vaporized dinner. That's your stomach telling you to eat food that requires chewing. And remember to swallow. You'll feel better in no time!
- PB

You Cannot Lose Weight Through Osmosis

When my wife and I were first married she asked me to buy her an exercise bike. If only she had an exercise bike, then she could look just like a model. I fell for it because who doesn't want to sleep with a model? She used the bike three times: twice for exercise and once on Halloween when she covered it with a white sheet and told all the Trick or Treaters it was a "ghost horse".

Some years later she purchased another piece of exercise equipment and weird ankle weights which was dutifully demonstrated on TV by a leggy model. If only she had *that* equipment, too, she was convinced she might look as good. Three weeks later UPS dropped it off. My wife used the equipment three times: twice for exercise and once to weigh down a tarp that I put over a pickup truck load of mulch so it wouldn't blow around on the highway.

Still, years later, she convinced me she needed a treadmill. She was certain the treadmill was the missing link in her quest to look like the leggy models she saw on TV. If only she could walk! Why, she would walk in the morning before work! In the evening before dinner! When she got up in the middle of the night to pee! She would walk her way to fitness! Already weakened by distractions like my high-pressure job and two children, I gave in. I purchased a treadmill and it worked like a charm - and it soon became an additional place in our bedroom to hang some of her clothes.

Time passed.

The exercise industry waited in anticipation for her next move.

Still nothing.

Then, just when I thought she had realized the error of her ways, she asked me for another treadmill. This time I balked. I argued. I pointed out her historical failures. It was useless. Eventually, I gave in and purchased a pretty pricey treadmill with water bottle holders, a two-speed built-in fan, a dozen different computerized training sequences, a tilt mode to simulate hills, an LED display that showed time, distance, calories, and the status of my 401k. I am happy to report my wife has broken her previous pattern by using her new high-tech "create your own leggy model machine" a total of ONE TIME! You cannot lose weight by looking at exercise equipment and thinking it is somehow making you thinner by owning it! - CD

Church of the Intelligent Robot

Artificial intelligence is being hotly-debated. Even Stephen Hawkings has questioned the ethics of AI. It has even begun to infiltrate religion.

Artificial intelligence and autonomous robots should be encouraged to become religious, according to Reverend Christopher Benek, associate pastor of Providence Presbyterian Church in Florida. He believes advanced forms of artificial intelligence should be welcomed into the Christian faith. "I don't see Christ's redemption limited to human beings," "It's redemption to all of creation, even AI. "

Are you frickin kidding me!

Yeah, that's all we need are religious robots. At first that sounds good, but can you imagine….I mean, first of all, They can't just be Christian. Think about all the denominations? They're all gonna' want their own. Do you really want the Jehovah's Witnesses to have a fleet of robot door knockers?

VOICE: "We know you are in there. You cannot escape the gospel."

You'll be able to recognize the Catholic Alter Bots. They'll be the only ones with a designated plug and play port on the back. At the Baptist church, the robot deacons will be the ones passing the bucket.

VOICE: "Sir, my calculations indicate that was not a 10% tithe. According to our records, your last W-2 indicates you make approximately $472 per week bring home. "

Soon enough, your own appliances will start to turn on you. I don't need my toaster witnessing to me at breakfast and reminding me that gluttony is a sin. I just wanna' eat my second honey bun and 6th strip of bacon in peace. Because when I get done, I will only have 30 minutes with the love droid before work and…, I swear to God, Toast bot if my robo-ho starts quoting Ephesians to me again, you won't be making toast, you will be toast. – PB

What if Jesus had been Fat?

Let me ask you: what if Jesus had been fat? Actually, we don't really know if he was chubby or not because history has only left us artist depictions - and artists always paint Jesus thin because it saves paint. What if Jesus had been as big as Michael Moore? The 'Last Supper' would have looked more like a weeknight at Golden Corral.

I don't think anyone wants to think the son of God was a fatty. It's probably sacrilegious just discussing it and right now some Holy Roly Poly priests in Rome are denouncing me. If Jesus had been fat could he have walked on water? And not just because there was a double-cheese pizza on the other side?

Then there's the crucifixion paradox. A fat Jesus could have never carried a big wooden cross anywhere and thin Romans could have never gotten a fat Jesus up on a cross. Read your history and you'll discover that in ancient Rome the heretics were never crucified because it was too difficult a process. Instead, the fat guys were told to roll themselves in a pool of whipped eggs and then had bread crumbs dumped all over them. After having baked in the hot sun for 6 hours, they were subsequently sent into the Coliseum disguised as fried mozzarella sticks just to confuse the Lions. – CD

Grateful for Dead Tech

D o you love music? Enough to listen to it forever? A Swedish company called Pause Custom Sound Systems presents the CataCombo, a music pumping customized coffin to turn your afterlife into the ultimate after party. There are three parts: The CataPlay music application which is powered by Spotify network, a 7-inch LCD display that all fits neatly into the headstone,and lastly, the customized coffin fitted with a pair of 2-way speakers, tweeters with external cooling and an 8-inch subwoofer. Isn't that the coolest?

Are you frickin' kidding me?

Have you ever had a song stuck in your head? Do you want it for eternity? What if you somehow can still hear it and the playlist is stuck on Gangnam Style? I mean, here I am, trapped in my brain in this underground hell and, thanks to these guys, I have two things to keep me company: The worms gnawing on my eyeballs and the red hot sound of Justin Bieber. If I wasn't dead I would kill myself again.

And, there's gonna' be an LCD screen on the tombstone showing you what's currently playing? How's my mom gonna' feel when she comes to visit me and it says Highway to Hell on the front of my tombstone? Is that supposed to be comforting to her?

What's next? Maybe you can hook me up with DeathFlix – the Netflix for Dead People. Probably playing that series Six Feet Under. Next up is Twilight. Ha ha, DeathFlix. You got me again.

This is beyond douchebag. This is beyond ridiculous. This is beyond a single lick of common sense. And as soon as this is public knowledge, it won't matter anyway because criminals will be robbing graves like crazy. They'll be rolling down the road with my coffin in the trunk blasting my Afterlife Snoop Dogg mix. So much for Rest in Peace, huh? – PB

Long Live Penmanship!

Years ago I installed Incredimail (long since gone) and trust me when I tell you this: it looked harmless at first but after you're forced to watch the annoying "mail butler" pop up a few hundred times I wanted to take my own life.

Did you know Incredimail is still available? It offers thousands of emoticons that you can drop into your messages. I don't even think I have 15 real emotions! Let's see: happy, sad, angry, and FUCK. Okay, I have four. Actually, I could substitute the first three for just FUCK because I can say FUCK whether I'm happy, sad, or angry. So where is the FUCK emoticon in Incredimail? There isn't one!

FUCK!

Before keyboards and email - when humans had to actually write letters and expose their penmanship - at least you could see what kind of person you were dealing with by their hand writing. Now, you don't know who you're throwing in with.

I know what some of you are saying: "Penmanship? Are you really going to go on a crusade for *penmanship*?"

Yes I am. And I don't want to see any of you roll your eyes in disbelief just because people have always told you that caring about "penmanship" is gay or something like that.

Penmanship is the art of writing with the hand and a writing instrument. When you take up a pen and write a letter in longhand you create a connection between your feelings, your spirit, and your thoughts that no keyboard can replicate. Pounding out the words you are reading right now through my keyboard look like any other shmuck's words. In order to make them matter, I have to try twice as hard to inject my unique humor and insight. (I know what you're thinking: so far, I'm failing.)

Not only have we lost penmanship but most people who send email messages are quite happy to allow their messages to be full of spelling and grammatical mistakes. It's almost as if somebody declared war on English the minute we figured out we could send email.

"Oh happy day! No more English for me now that I have a new way to send letters and forward every stupid thing somebody sends me. Oh Lord thank you for lifting the burden of having to punctuate! Oh God thank you for erasing the necessity to spell! I can dangle participles without fear and create run-on sentences without trepidation. I am free to appear - - illiterate!"

When did appearing to be illiterate become cool? Why would anyone want to be thought *less* of? I can understand taking shortcuts on Twitter or even in text messages where there are time and space limitations. But, not in email messages. We have spell checkers and grammar checkers designed to make you look good.

So, why does it matter? It matters because your life should be quality, not mediocrity. If you want mediocrity then move to Hoboken, New Jersey. Trust me on this: I've been there. - CD

Man vs. Animals: How Much Competition do you Want?

It turns out that a type of cell found in the human central nervous system that had previously been thought little more than a sort of "housekeeper" cell is actually really important for cognitive function. How did we learn this? A team of researchers used them to create mouse-human hybrids. And the mice became significantly smarter. They are now testing larger rodents and animals. They feel this research could be useful in treating diseases such as multiple sclerosis. That is just great news!

Are you fricking kidding me!

We're all gonna' die! You're giving animals human brain cells that make em smarter? What, the robots weren't enough competition for you guys? We got fewer jobs, robots doing jobs, immigrants doing jobs and now you're telling me that one day I might have to compete with animals? Because you know this won't stop with mice. One day, I may have to compete with a cheetah in the workplace. How awkward is that gonna' be in the lobby?

"Say, you there...human. You applying for the job?"

"Ummm...yep."

"Well, I got three cubs in the den and I really need this job so, I suggest you leave now or the next time you see me I'll be leaping off your hedges."

And, while giving mice more intelligence may seem fairly harmless, bear in mind that at one point they will realize what a mouse trap is and it will dawn on them just how many of their kind we have killed. There won't be a pest control man on the planet without a bounty on his head from the mouse community. That's ok, Mr Scientist. You go ahead. Make your animal hybrids. But don't blame me when you come home just in time to catch your wife in bed with a Panda Bear. I'm sorry honey....but he's just so cute. I had to do him. – PB

Earthling: Take Me to Your Latte!

If space men ever land on Earth, I think the first thing they're going to do is execute the man who invented the "Clapper" as an example to all of humanity just how freakin' lazy we are. The light switch is 3 feet away from your bed yet you're such a tub of lard you won't even get up and walk over to it to shut the damn lamp off. Honestly, I'm with the aliens on this.

As a matter of fact, I'm betting they will also vaporize whoever came up with the "Snuggie", the "Grill Daddy", "Debbie Meyer Green Bags" (well, they know who to kill there), the "Potty Patch", "Aqua Globes", the "Buxton Bag", "Point 'n Paint", and "Mighty Putty". Actually, I wouldn't be surprised if the aliens – through their advanced technology – resurrected dead Billy Mays just to kill him a second time.

Aliens are *not* going to come in peace. They are going to land crabby with a chip on their shoulder – or whatever body part sits below their heads – if they have heads. The main problem with preparing to fight off space invaders is we don't know what they'll look like. They might look like tacos with legs. They might look like Lindsey Lohan with three eyes. I just hope they don't navigate their space ship as badly as she drives.

Aliens will have studied us and will know one of our true weaknesses: we believe anything we read on the Internet and assume it is true. That's why before initiating any offensive they are going to run several covert missions to Earth for one reason: to win the bloggers over to their side.

Typical Blogger, Circa 2000

Many bloggers – not all – but many should never have been allowed to have a laptop and broadband. A lot of bloggers will write the stupidest things – and repeat even stupider ones. We used to have a name for them. Oh yeah: Village Idiots. Many bloggers have no idea what they are talking about because they are short on facts and long on speculation. Yet, they continue to clog up the Internet with all sorts of misinformation and disinformation.

That's why bloggers are an easy target for aliens. The aliens will most likely disguise themselves as someone the bloggers would trust – like a Starbucks barista. Have you ever noticed the close relationship between a blogger and a barista? Every barista knows every blogger and what they like to drink. You can even change out the baristas and bloggers – move them to random stores – and the switched-out baristas will still know what the switched-out bloggers like to drink. It's uncanny. Bloggers and baristas speak in some strange language of "Grandes", "Cinnamon Dolce Frappuccinos", "Ethos" water, and "Tazo" teas.

Besides bloggers being mentally "pliable", there's another reason why space goons might very well infiltrate as baristas at Starbucks: wireless Internet. While bloggers are sitting in front of their laptops drinking their Café Au Lait, the invaders will transmit their mind-control to the bloggers' laptops via the convenient Wi-Fi hotspot. One minute the bloggers will be uploading their latest column to meathead.blogspot.com and the next minute their screens will be turned into an excel spreadsheet that contains subliminal messages beamed by Captain Green Genitals from the planet Gallorpinax.

So, that's how it will start: the mother ship will communicate through motherboards. Bloggers will create a first wave of death by bashing in the heads of citizens using their laptop computers. There are over 16,000 Starbucks in 49 countries and 11,000 of them are right here in the United States. Imagine what a first strike by bloggers would do? 16,000 x 10 customers per store = 160,000 dead within the first few minutes of the alien attack – and that's not even counting store personnel.

Think about the next time you're in Starbucks, human. - CD

Starbucks Euphemisms for Masturbation

Flickin' the Bean

Spicing the Pumpkin Latte

Mixing the Pike's Place

Getting the Gluten out of the Bagel

Warming up the Dark Roast

Percolating her Cooterchino

Scruffin' My Scone

Manhandling the Macchiato

Whippin' the White Cholcolate

Fappin' the Frappuccino

Entering the Well with the Ethos

Feeling Good about a Fair Trade Tickle – PB, CD

Man Conquers Space

Black Hole Terminology

"General Relativity" - this describes what happens when cousins and other relations show up at your house for Thanksgiving.

"Escape Velocity" - how quickly a husband can get out of spending time with his mother-in-law during general relativity.

"Apparent Horizon" - The furthest you can view one of your wife's parents driving away because you insulted them during general relativity.

"Scale Factor" - a measurement of how dry the skin is on the turkey your sister-in-law baked too long on Thanksgiving

"Point of no Return" - the moment the general relativity comes in your front door and takes off their coats. - CD

The Great Debate:
Washcloth or No?

Have you ever done something a certain way your whole life and then get into a relationship and all of the sudden your partner questions how you do something? Something you might not even think about.

Guys…please back me up on this one…

So, my wife and I have been married a year now and she asked me the other day, " don't you use a washcloth in the shower?"

And I'm like, "uhhhhhh…..no."

"Well, how do you wash? "

"With soap."

"You mean you just rub the soap on your body? "

"Well, yeah."

"So, how do you wash your ass?"

And I'm like, "Who I vote for and how I wash my ass are none of your business. "

"So, you're putting the soap on your ass?"

"Well, I'm not putting my hand on it."

She said, "That's disgusting, you should use a wash cloth. It exfoliates your skin and then I don't have to use soap you put on your ass."

I said, "A) It's soap, how do you get soap dirty? Unless I'm washing my ass and drop a deuce on the soap, it's fine. But speaking of that, how do you wash your ass with a washcloth? "

"Well, just like you would with the soap.

"And your feet? "

"With the washcloth."

"Which comes first? Because either you wash your ass first and put ass on your feet or you wash your feet first and get athlete's ass."

Yeah, I think I'll stick with the soap. – PB

One Day at the Cheese Oracle

A follower: Oh holy oracle of Cheese: I come to you on my knees seeking advice.

The Oracle of Cheese: I cannot see you my son for I have no eyes. Please come closer.

A follower: Uh...you don't have any ears, either. How is it you hear me but cannot see me?

The Oracle of Cheese: I see your spirit in my mind's eye.

A follower: Yean, but you said you don't have any eyes.

The Oracle of Cheese: It's a figure of speech.

A follower: Wait a second. I hear you but you don't have a mouth, either. Is this a trick?

The Oracle of Cheese: Alright, look: you're kind of pissing me off. I have a very busy schedule today. The people from Kraft want to meet with me about a Macaroni and Cheese issue, the Mexicans are all upset because of some damn Taco problem, the Sargento family is still nagging me, and you are kneeling there just yanking my chain, kid!

A follower: *I never realized I had so many doubts. I liked it better when we used to seek advice and guidance from the Oracle of Little Debbie Snacks.*

The Oracle of Cheese: *Again with the Little Debbie regrets? That bitch! It's because I'm fat, isn't it?*

A follower: *No, I never said that.*

The Oracle of Cheese: *You didn't have to. I'm made up of a little protein and a lot of fat. Everyone knows that about cheese. Just look at me: I'm hideous. Not like Little Debbie. Oh no....she's FULL of carbs and yet hasn't aged a day in 50 years!*

A follower: *I'm going now.*

The Oracle of Cheese: *(shouting) Fine! Go back to your false idol! Your Little Debbie Oracle Whore Bitch! I don't need you!* - CD

Please, Don't Send Me There

The most confusing place a man can be sent is the feminine hygiene aisle. First of all, there is more space for tampons than motor oil. How can there even be that many choices? They have the Pearls. Is that a formal tampon for high class events? Yes, I am bleeding but I'm doing it with style! And Radiant tampons? What is it radiating? Are they glow in the dark? That way if you get up in the middle of the night you can see what you're doing? You just open your bathrobe and it's like a little coochi flashlight.

And they always make it out to be some technological breakthrough likes it's the new I-Tampon from Apple. Now with an MP3 player. Make your period better with I-tunes! Look, how much technology can go into cotton and plastic. How much better can you really make it?

Then they have the pads with wings? WINGS? What the hell do they need wings for? Have you ever seen an aerodynamic coochie? I would like to. I would fly those friendly skies. "This is your captain speaking. May be some turbulence ahead."

And in the commercials, they're always at the beachThe last thing my wife wants to do when she's on her period is go anywhere. She wants a recliner, the remote and the kids to shut the hell up. The beach, really?

First of all, I've seen enough jaws movies to know this is a VERY bad idea! The last place I wanna' be with my wife bleeding is in the ocean with sharks.

Second, and what I really don't understand; A tampon is supposed to be absorbent. They show you how absorbent they are in the commercials by pouring like a gallon of water in it. And now you wanna' get in the ocean? Ummmm.....that's water. I would think as soon as you got in the ocean it would go POOOOF!

I guess the good news is, if you go to far out you could just pull the string and it turns into a floatation device. At least until the sharks come.

What's next. I guess you can use your period as an excuse to go skydiving. You know where the rip cord is....right? POOOOF! – PB

Interactive: please take this time to just try yelling it once and see how good it feels. Try it several ways as you read. Find your own outrage. Thank me later!

.

The Worst Condiment

Mustard is like the codependent condiment. You'll dip anything in ketchup or ranch …..fries, chicken, fish, chips… but mustard gets two things: the hot dog and the pretzel. Let me put it in perspective; if you had a hot date and the girl said you can get on these boobies but only if you put ketchup on em, you'd be like….ummmmm…alright then. But if she said, yeah, you can get on these but they're gonna' be doused in mustard, you'd pull the car over right there. Get out, ya freak. And ya know why? It's not even the taste.

It's the fact that no matter how careful you are, an hour later you will look down and find mustard stain on your fingers. You could be wearing new work gloves when you make that hot dog and somehow, when you take em off, there will be mustard there. And no matter how long you wash it, suck on it, take sandpaper to it, you aren't getting the mustard off. It's like an ex wife or husband. No matter how much you want the stain of the past to go away….here I am. – PB

A Short History of Condiments

Mean Mr. Mustard

You can thank the Romans for coming up with mustard. They mixed unfermented grape juice, known as "must" with ground mustard seeds (called sinapis) to make "burning must", mustum ardens — hence "must ard."

At the time, the hot dog had not been invented so the Romans put mustard on the next best thing: a live goat. Getting the mustard on the goat was easy. Getting the goat to walk into a bun the size of a Subaru was not. Actually, it was frustrating which is how the term "get your goat" originated which means to make one annoyed or angry.

Having had their fill of mustard-coated live goats, the Romans gave the knowledge of mustard to the monks of St. Germain des Pres in Paris in the 10th century. Dijon, France became *Mustard Central* by the 13th century and by 1777 the most famous Dijon mustard makers of them all, Grey-Poupon, was established. The hyphenated brand name comes from Maurice Grey and Auguste Poupon who were terribly distinguished in their day. If they knew their little mustard company would one day be owned by Kraft Foods - most famous for a box of macaroni and cheese - they would have put their heads on a guillotine and pulled the rope themselves.

Luckily, Grey and Poupon did not live to see their Dijon mustard upstaged by some brash American mustard that looked like a melted yellow Crayola crayon. Yet, that's what happened thanks to Robert Timothy French and his sons Francis and George.

French's Cream Salad Mustard debuted in 1904 at the St. Louis World's Fair where attendees found it went quite well with hot dogs. Sure, live goats were also offered along with the hot dogs but in the end, the fair goers overwhelmingly chose hot dogs over live goats and to this day, nobody puts mustard on a live goat.

Unless you're lost and stranded in the mountains of Afghanistan. Then, all bets are off.

Your Food Goes to the Mayo Clinic

Historians think mayonnaise was brought back to France from Menorca, Spain after Louis-François-Armand du Plessis de Richelieu was victorious over British forces there in 1756.

Whatever happened to rape and pillage? This guy wins a battle and all he wants as the spoils of battle is the local sandwich spread? Being what it is, Richelieu brought "salsa mahonesa" back with him to France.

135

Historians can't quite settle on how the Spanish name for mayo morphed into the French *mayonnaise* but it's a known fact that men in the French Court used mayonnaise to keep their fashionably powdered wigs attached to the crowns of their balding heads. Unfortunately, after a long day lounging around looking like a gay mime with makeup and dainty shoes, they began to smell like the inside of a bad egg salad sandwich. To mask the odor, men of the French Court were often surrounded by French pastries and fresh baked goods, dictated by Marie Antoinette who famously said, "Let them eat cake." It was not a political statement about the peasants. She just wanted the room deodorized by the smell of petit fours, éclairs, croissants, and beignets.

Hellman's Mayonnaise started as a homemade condiment at the New York City delicatessen of German immigrant Richard Hellmann in 1905. Actually, it was his wife's recipe and her knack for making mayo charmed so many customers that the Hellmanns began to offer it for sale in "wooden boats" that were used for weighing butter.

The Hellmanns worked together for many years until one day when Mrs. Hellman found Richard in bed with another woman ready to have sexual intercourse. More specifically, he was ready to make bacon, she said "let us" because she was one hot "tomato." When Mrs. Hellmann walked into the bedroom and saw this, she tossed a bowl of mayonnaise on the lovers and that's how the BLT - or Bacon, Lettuce, and Tomato sandwich was born.

Today, mayonnaise is abused millions of times-a-day throughout the world as it is put on a myriad of incongruent foods that scream to just be left alone. But, the most egregious use of mayonnaise must sit with the Europeans who actually serve it with French fries. The irony is overwhelming since the French get credit for naming mayonnaise yet now are reduced to using it on a product that is not at all French, but American.

C'est la vie.

Playing Catch Up with Ketchup's Past

By all accounts, the Chinese came up with the original ketchup. Their version was a combination of pickled fish and spices called "ketsiap." The recipe worked its way over to Malaysia where British explorers found it. By 1740, the British were using it on a regular basis. Oddly, it wasn't until around 1800 the recipe changed from using pickled fish to being tomato-based.

How exactly does pickled fish get replaced by tomatoes? (Sure, most of us would gladly pass on more pickled fish in lieu of tomatoes if offered it at Thanksgiving dinner.) But, how does a cook consciously decide he or she is going to change a recipe so drastically? After much consternation, I realized that just like Kevin Bacon is connected to everything in the world by six degrees, tomatoes are also connected to everything in the world by six degrees.

The Six Degrees of Tomatoes

Pickled fish easily becomes tomatoes in six steps:

1. Pickled fish was often eaten by sailors.
2. Barrels held pickled fish on ships.
3. Ships often encounter violent storms.
4. Violent storms toss ships from bow to stern
5. A state of disorder or confusion is known as topsy turvy.
6. Topsy Turvy® is the name of an upside down tomato planter

Pickled Fish = Tomatoes

I know what you're thinking: I'm a freakin' genius. - CD

**One Day the Ketchup God 'Tomaton' Will
Return to Earth and Destroy All the Mayonnaise**

In Grill We Trust

The human boddy is pretty cool 'cause it can turn food into energy and farts. Now, I'm not a big science guy but even I have to admit that's amazin'! And the energy part is cool, too! As a small businessman and soul proprieter of Cooter Burger in Blue Ball, Arkansaw, I am often asked by customers what is my seekrit to making a great burger. It's simple: I season my cows while they are still alive. Ofen, I will go out into the pasture at night and shake salt, pepper, and a few other choice seasonings on the cow while it's sleeping. This way, the spices have a chance to really seep into the meet.

Seasoning live animals can be a little dangerous because they're not that dumb and realize you're just trying to make them taste better 'cause you're 'gonna' smack 'em over the head with a baseball bat eventually. This may cause some premature hard feelings between you and your cows. To avoid this, it is best to disguise yourself as a haystack. I had to make my own haystack costume since I have never seen one at Walmart – even at Halloween time.

One nice thing about having a haystack costume is you can always put it on and say to the misses, "Hey? Wanna' have a roll in the hay?" If I've been out seasoning the cows, she'll usually tell me I'm a pig and I should take a shower. I love that sexy talk!

Anyway, now that you know my seekrit to makin' a good hamburger, I hope you will be very sukksessful in grilling burgers and stuff. My last suggesti on for you is get a good grill. A real man's grill. One without that pussy propane shit like the  haugty taughties in Chenal Valley. If you don't use hickory or at least charcoal, I will personally kick your ass.

On second thought, even charcoal in bags is kind of gay. Real men use chips, chunks, or logs. Oh, and none of them sissy long, plastic bic fire starters. If you don't have the balls to hold a match, don't even offer me a hot dog.

So, I hope I've helped in your pursuit of making man food. And please stop by soon for a

Cooter Burger the next time you drive through
beautiful downtown Blue Ball, Arkansaw.
— Yur friend, Bocephus Cooter

Why Do We Say That?
Part I

Ever considered the meaning behind colloquialisms and idioms we use on a regular basis? We say it so casually but what the hell does it mean?

"Beating around the bush…"

This implies you are not directly beating the bush. And why the hell would anyone "beat the bush"? Unless you're using that to give masturbation directions it's stupid. And even then it seems violent.

"A penny saved is a penny earned…."

No…a penny saved is yet another thing in the bottom of my junk drawer taking up space I could use for something really valuable. Who the hell saves pennies? You know who? 5 year olds. They save em up for two years and at 7 they realize they saved enough to get a snickers and a mountain dew. As soon as I get pennies I just throw em on the street. You know the person that finds em needs em more than you do. They can get a bottle of vodka for about 287 of those. So….help cirrhosis and throw a penny down.

"It's always in the last place you look."

How profound is that? Really? The last place I look? No shit because when I find it I stop looking dumbass. Why would it be the middle place I looked? Like I'm gonna' find that shit and say....you know....looking for this has been so much fun I think I'll keep doing it!

"Giving head " (felatio)

This is one of the dumbest ones ever. You're not giving head. You have a penis in your mouth. It's more like giving mouth or sharing tongue. Or just call it what it is....and that's NOT a BLOW JOB which is even dumber. You know who invented this? Women who didn't know how to give mouth.

If you're down there blowing on it like it's a birthday candle then A) You're probably an idiot and B) you are likely near being punched on principal alone. - PB

144

Why Do We Say That?
Part II

"Break a leg."

Somewhere in the world of actors, saying good luck was imagined to cause the opposite so people went with break a leg. Why break a leg? Couldn't you have just said….hope it's ok. Or maybe things will do nicely this evening? But break a leg?

You may as well say…..so you're performing tonight? Yeah! Well, I hope you catch on fire and burn to death and right before you take your last superheated breath you see a tv screen with your mom doing midget porn. I mean, shit….they should have the best performance ever. Probably based on the endorphins of beating ☐he hell out of the person who said that stupid shit.

"A bird in the hand is worth two in the bush."

Hey….bird shit is terrible. I don't want any birds in my hand and if I see someone next to my bush holding birds I'm calling the cops.

"Absence makes the heart grow fonder."

Fonder of the person who's replaced you in my life, maybe.

"Sooner rather than later."

If you're in such a damn rush, why did you waste everybody's time saying all that? Wouldn't "soon" have sufficed?

"Everything happens for a reason."

This is just the stupid shit people say to you when they don't know what else to say. My mom was just brutally murdered by a group of wild chimpanzees. Well, everything happens for a reason. Yes….like the ass whipping I am about to give you.

"The way to man's heart is through his stomach"

Only if his penis somehow moved there.

– PB

Why Men Love the #10 Can

I'm a sucker for a #10 can. Actually, a big fan. Recently, I was talking with someone and mentioned a "#10 can" to which he simply responded with an inquisitive look and said, "What's that?"

I was shocked.

I thought everyone knew what a #10 can was. So, I began to describe it: "Well, a #10 can is, uh, you know those industrial size cans of food they sell at Sam's Club. The big ones? Well, that's a #10 can."

He accepted my explanation but was obviously underwhelmed by the whole concept (an expected response from someone who didn't even make it out of Cub Scouts. He will most likely be one of the first to be eaten by the zombies at the appropriate time since he has no survival skills whatsoever.)

A #10 can is the biggest can you can buy something in. It holds 12 cups or 24 servings of whatever you put in it. Sure, there are other sizes: #1, #2, #3, #5, #211, #300, and #303. But, they are all inferior to the mighty #10 can.

Famous foods that come out of #10 cans include that vanilla pudding so often served at cheap buffets. Yep: the next time you're spooning down a plateful of that sweet slop remember it once lived in a #10 can as do most institutional foods served en masse to hungry folks who are generally not expecting filet mignon yet are grateful for two servings of meatloaf.

Out of curiosity, I did a quick Google search to see how the #10 can might be serving humanity today. I wasn't surprised to find "Mountain House #10 Can Spaghetti with Meat and Sauce" and "Mountain House #10 Can Beef Stroganoff with Noodles", both available at Amazon.com. I think you can see how including "#10 can" in the name of the product only enhances the promised flavor.

The #10 can is truly an engineering marvel. It is just the right size for so many utilities. Besides preserving large amounts of carbohydrates for years-at-a-time, #10 cans are next to camping Godliness. A survivalist could use them for practically everything: cooking, hauling water, holding zombie teeth (hey: we all need our trophies), a quick 'n dirty dinner bell, and even storing powdered Moos Milk.

Trust in the #10 can. It will serve you well.
– CD

T-Rex Sex

A woman was left embarrassed after she was forced to go to a hospital to remove a toy from her private parts. The woman was forced to seek help from doctors after she was unable to remover her son's toy dinosaur from her private parts. The woman said that she was pleasuring herself with the child's T-Rex dinosaur, and it became logged inside her body. The doctor said, "I don't advise inserting children's toys during sexual activity." Are you frickin kidding me!

Who the hell is this judgmental quack? You don't advise inserting children's toys during sex? Just like PETA, all you wanna' do is take away everyone's fun. All you moms out there, back me up. What's better than getting GI Joe in the foxhole? Every mom wants to take He-Man to Castle Vajayskull. And you know damn well that, at least once, you took off his cape and utility belt and helped the Dark Knight get in the Bat Cave. Hell, some of you adventurous ladies may have even let him drive the batmobile in. But, we all know the best of best is that moment you can look down and say, Welcome to Jurassic Park. You get a couple drinks in a hot mama and they all wanna' put a t-rex in the tootoo. RAWR! Seriously.

Lady, come on. I mean, I get being horny but a T-Rex? Maybe, I'm crazy but I would think that, of all the items in my house, T-Rex would be pretty damn far down the list. You see, this is where PETA CAN help. Can you guys tell her about vegetables? You didn't have ANYTHING cylindrical? You know, like a PENIS? And, if you're man's junk is shaped like a T-Rex, A) That's horrifying and B) he likely needs antibiotics. Maybe he's the one that needs to be going to the ER. Of all the people I feel bad for in this equation, it's the doctor. I guess, the good news is, at least the T-Rex wasn't stuck in the tar pit, if you get my drift. - PB

Man vs. Toaster

In 1989, when screensavers were new and cool and actually functioned to save screens, there was a series called the "Flying Toasters". Remember that? It was a screensaver that featured airborne toasters with wings that criss-crossed your screen along with pieces of toast in order to keep your monitor from burning in. I've never been comfortable with the concept of flying toasters. This is wrong on all levels. Appliances should not be able to travel and I sometimes wonder if the Flying Toasters screensaver wasn't more of a foreshadowing of things to come.

Think about it: which appliance in your home exposes you more easily to electricity than your toaster? "According to industry sources, nearly 3,300 residential fires occur each year because of faulty toasters and toaster ovens, resulting in $25 million worth of property damage," says accessmylibrary.com.

In 1996, *The Baltimore Sun* reported that Bethlehem Steel was "...fined $3,640 four months after Raymond Pritts was electrocuted when he touched a defective toaster oven in a lunchroom at the Sparrows Point plant."

The blog *Schrodinger's Kitten* notes: "...7 Americans are electrocuted every year by their faithful kitchen bread-incinerators, and personally, if I'm going to put my life on the line, I want more out of it than some singed wheat products."

Okay, so that's....8 for sure.

Look: don't get bogged down in the facts.

The facts can be misleading because that's what the toasters want you to believe! They will sit there all sort of friendly with their two big slots for bread and act like nothing's wrong. It's like the aliens from space who might disguise themselves as Starbucks baristas. The machines will do the same thing: come as friends and then turn their deadly microchips on you and then WHO WILL BE TOAST?

You, my friend. You. – CD

An Insidious Flying Toaster with Wings Retracted and Antenna Poised to Receive Instructions from the Robotic Collective.

Rats! Another Bomb!

Men are so ingenius! During World War II, exploding rats were developed to be used against the Germans. I'm not kidding. The Brits took dead rats and filled them with plastic explosives. "The idea that when the rats were shoveled along with coal into boilers, they would explode, causing significant damage. However, the first shipment of carcasses was intercepted by the Germans, and the plan was dropped," according to thecontaminated.com.

The Rat Bomb may have been a complete failure but memories are long in the rat world. As humans, we kid about being caught up in the "rat race" with our jobs, busy lives, and commitments.

But, if rats are given the chance, they will strike back with force and you'll *really* be in a rat race – for your life! – CD

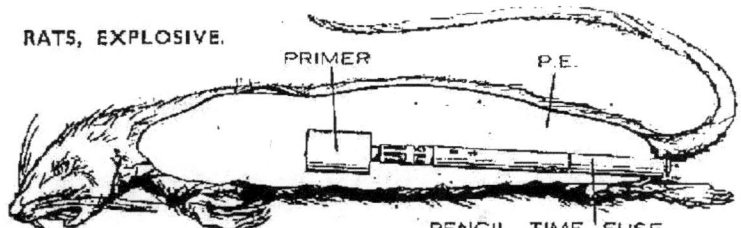

RATS, EXPLOSIVE.

PRIMER

P.E.

PENCIL TIME FUSE

A rat is skinned, the skin being sewn up and filled with P.E. to assume the shape of a dead rat. A Standard No. 6 Primer is set in the P.E. Initiation is by means of a short length of safety fuse with a No. 27 detonator crimped on one end and a copper tube igniter on the other end, or, as in the case of the illustration above, a P.T.F. with a No. 27 detonator attached. The rat is then left amongst the coal beside a boiler and the flames initiate the safety fuse when the rat is thrown on to the fire, or, as in the case of the P.T.F, a Time Delay is used.

Caption Couldn't Be Stupider Than the Truth: A "Rat Bomb" Per British Secret Service Instructions

~~Men~~ Infants at Work

Washington State is Letting New Parents Bring Their Babies to Work Whenever They Want. That's right: state officials enacted the "Infant-at-Work Program Policy," which allows new parents or legal guardians working at the Traffic Safety Commission to bring their babies to the office. The kids don't have to pass any kind of quiet test. They just have to be at least 6 weeks old. The babies are allowed to keep coming in until they are either six months old, or they start to crawl; Officials said research proves that allowing parents to stay with their infants "supports critical bonding, healthy infant brain development, and parental well-being."

YOU GOTTA BE FRICKIN KIDDING ME! Now tell me how you can deny Satan wants your workplace? Not only, am I gonna' have to sit at my desk pedaling a bike but now I'm gonna' have to do it while listening to some colicky newborn baby scream like two cats banging at midnight while someone is running their nails down a chalkboard and jabbing an ice pick in the side of my head. The only way this workplace could get any worse is if it smelled like…..HOLY…..you ever walked into a daycare for the first time? You know, before you go noseblind to the fact it smells like mac and cheese served in a diaper with a fresh load of ass raisins? And Suzy cubemate is all excited to show you....LOOK! It's avocado green!

You think he's getting too much iron? Lady, you're about to get some iron in the form of a stapler too the face if you and the poop paying slot machine you're holding don't get the hell outta my cube! Can't you see I'm working out here? By the way, gimme one of those diapers. I got a hardcore case of swamp ass. – PB

A Short History of Cats

A long time ago, aliens from outer space landed their ships on the Egyptian pyramids. This was fully documented in the 1994 movie *Stargate*, starring Kurt Russell. If you know anything about Kurt Russell's career, you know that he only does movies based on reality like the 1989 cop movie *Tango & Cash*, 1982's *The Thing* (where an alien being occupies bodies of men and dogs living in Antarctica), *Captain Ron*, the 1992 true-to-life movie about sea life, and the stunning 1981 documentary about American hero, Snake Plisken, the man who saved the President of the United States in *Escape from New York*.

Kurt Russell is kind of a God when it comes to movie realism.

Anyway, when aliens first visited earth they brought cats with them as a food source. Aliens snacked on cats often and this delight in felines led to the phrase "cat got your tongue" meaning a delicious morsel of catness was still lingering on their taste buds.

Cats did not enjoy being a food source for aliens because these interplanetary visitors preferred to eat them alive. Hence, if you've ever looked into a cat's eyes, they usually have that "freaked out" look. This is a genetically transferred pose which cats developed as a response to looking at the pinching mandibles attached to the alien's mouth.

Eventually, the cats fled from Egypt while the aliens were busy at an offsite job creating the statues on Easter Island. Since cats aren't Kosher (true) they couldn't leave when the Pharaoh let the Jews exit. So, the great *Cat Exodus* occurred sometime after all the Hebrews fled with their unleavened bread, leaving behind for the cats only leavened or high-caloric bread to eat. During this time of plentiful carbs, the first instances of really ornery, fat, and sassy cats showed itself and hence, the term "fat cat" evolved, meaning one who has a lot of bread...or is very rich.

Cats roamed the earth in search of a place they could live peacefully, out of reach from their former owners, the space aliens. Instead of trekking across the Middle East westward, they jumped on a light sailboat which became known as a "catamaran." Through wind and rain, sun, and darkness they pushed forward until they finally landed in China.

Big mistake.

The Chinese really took a liking to cats because they were plentiful, easy to catch, and they tasted better in Moo Goo Gai Pan than chicken. Of course, the chickens resented the incursion and immediately appealed to the Federal government to seal off the borders. Alas, the Chinese Feds did nothing and cats crossed the border into China and became the meals chickens didn't want to become.

Soon afterwards, Korea asked China if it could have some cats so it could breed them for their meals as well. The Koreans changed the spelling of "cat" to "kat" because, well....it's KOREA and they are weird like that. Eventually, the Koreans came to like kat so much in their meals, they began to develop snack foods. The most well known one is a candy bar. You've probably heard of it: the "Kit Kat" bar.

Kats and cats eventually moved West again, this time toward Europe. During the Middle Ages black cats were discriminated against and thought to be evil and having thrown in with the Devil. It was a difficult time for "cats of color" and they had to fight long and hard for equal rights with dogs.

Finally, the decision was made to come to America where they could be free. During passage across the ocean, cats would stow away on boats often unknown to the crews. This was probably a good thing because crossing the ocean was an arduous and time consuming task and if those salty sailors on board had known about all the pussies waiting below, it probably would have led to complete bedlam.

The first cats actually landed at Plymouth Rock and immediately mistook it for a giant piece of kitty litter. The subsequent confusion led to the *Great Cat Constipation of 1620* which saw hundreds of felines walking very awkwardly through portions of New England in search of a giant box with kitty litter on the scale of the aforementioned boulder.

Eventually, the cats were led into the wilderness by a friendly Indian who showed them the ways of the New World. The cats reciprocated by scratching his eyes out and tearing his flesh. Fortunately, the Indian was rescued by fellow tribesmen who brought him back to their healer. The medicine man placed his hands above the injured Indian, waving them ever so slowly back and forth to diagnose his dilemma. This process later became known as a "cat scan".

Cats have come a long way since their days as food for alien beings from another planet. They have progressed up the cultural ladder and fought hard for their place in our society which is usually an abandoned freezer in the basement of some crackpot. - CD

Suck it, Turtle!

Ever since I was a small child I've been told the world is poised on the constant verge of annihilation. It used to be the Russians had nukes aimed at us and the U.S. had nukes aimed at them. One false move and Earth was a mushroom cloud. Today, things are much different: Russia still has nukes aimed at us, we still have nukes aimed at them, but China has nukes aimed at both of us, all three of us have nukes aimed at North Korea, Israel has nukes aimed at Iran and Iran swears all it has is a nuclear power plant aimed at producing electricity.

Right.

Maybe the end of the world won't be ignited from some external event but, rather, from a manmade threat - like nuclear missiles. A recent estimate by the Federation of American Scientists pegged the amount of nuclear warheads on Earth at 23,000. And if you're really keeping track, Russia has 13,000 and we have 9,400. It used to be worse: in 1986, the world had 70,000 nukes.

Beginning in the 1950s into the 1980s, the government had a very simple solution to surviving a nuclear attack: "Duck and Cover". The Federal Civil Defense Administration launched a giant media campaign headed by a cartoon mascot named "Bert the Turtle". There were comic books, pamphlets, recordings, public service announcements, and more informing the public that should a nuclear missile be headed toward them, just duck under the nearest desk or picnic table and cover your head.

But, why a turtle? According to one Duck and Cover movie poster: "He's smart, but he has his shelter on his back...you must learn to find shelter." Well, that's great: foist a mascot on the public who has nothing vested in seeking shelter. What a great example. The freakin' turtle is going to be fine because he's already got protection. As for the rest of you, well...you'll have to learn to run fast. Plus, Bert's a damn turtle - one of the slowest animals in the world. What kind of model is that for petrified people desperately seeking shelter to avoid an incoming missile? - CD

Dude, Your Breath Smells Like a Gym

A man was arrested, charged and convicted of fraud after selling a bag full of dirty socks as marijuana, prosecutors in Michigan said. The incident began when a couple was looking to buy a pound of marijuana. They gave 33-year-old Michael Suarez, $2,800 for a bag stuffed with dirty socks. Suarez is facing a prison sentence of up to 7 years. He was arrested while driving away from the couple for running a stop sign.

Are you frickin kidding me! You arrested the dude who sold the socks? What is that charge? Felony foot covering? This guy shouldn't be in jail, he should be in Hollywood receiving an Academy Award for Best Actor. You wanna' arrest someone; arrest that couple for 1st degree stupidity. Can you imagine how that transaction went down? "Is that some of that real, sticky icky?" "Oh it's icky, alright, ese" "Is this that Doprah Winfrey?" "No, gringo." "Is it LaBong James?" "No, ese. Catch a whiff of this." And then they gave him $2800. These two slack-jawed, knuckle-draggers sniffed up a bag filled with rank ass, athlete's feet stuffed socks and thought it smelled like some of that Alexander GramBag.

They're so stupid I'm surprised they didn't die trying to smoke a tube sock. Why would the police even interfere with this? Do you want these people to get another shot at buying weed? Think of how dumb they are now? They were much better off with a bag of socks. At least they would've had warm feet. I mean, it IS Michigan. And anyone who could mistake a nasty bag of socks for some of that Scotty Rippen or Bret BOWLema has at least a 50/50 shot of freezing to death because, what they thought they were snorting was an 8-ball of Columbian cocaine but turned out to be a snowball.
- PB

We like our Hamburgers

Symptomatic of this is just how big hamburgers at fast food restaurants grew over the years. At one point, Rally's had a "triple cheeseburger", Burger King had the Whopper®, and Hardees had a ⅔ pound Monster Thickburger®. Even so, in the general scheme of things, these are all small potatoes, fried please.

Go to Denny's Beer Barrel Pub in Clearfield, Pennsylvania. This place features a two, three, six, fifteen, and fifty pound hamburger (requires 24 hour notice) and a 100 pound hamburger called the, "Beer Barrel Main Event Burger" (requires 72 hour notice).

You don't eat something that big. You pray to it and ask it to smite annoying people from PETA.

Me? I'm holding out for someone to introduce a live cow baked into a bun the size of a Subaru.

All we do is think about food. Have you ever heard of Gomez's Hamburger? No, it's not a new menu item from Sonic. It's actually a protoplanetary nebula discovered in 1985 by Arturo Gomez.

The man named it after his dinner!!

This should trouble you.

166

When you view the photograph of Gomez' Hamburger, "The 'hamburger buns' are light reflecting off dust, and the 'patty' is the dark band of dust in the middle, " says Wikipedia.

Why is all this talk of food relevant to the end-of-the-world? Because one of the scenarios for the big goodbye is worldwide global famine - death by starvation. The good news: the only people who might survive are those who are padding themselves with the human equivalent of whale blubber. The bad news: a natural explosion of enough fat people under the right circumstances and we could see a domino effect which might be deadlier than a nuclear reaction. – CD

Two All Beef Patties, Special Sauce, Lettuce, Cheese, Pickles, Onions on a Sesame Seed Black Hole

Church's Donation Plate Replaced with Panties!

A gentleman's club in Guelph, Ontario, is holding church services right on the stage next to the stripper pole. The Manor, as the club is called, held services for the first time on Easter. Jack Ninaber and his wife Sharon decided they would host a Christian fellowship service at the unconventional space in order to bring religion to those who don't feel comfortable seeking it out. Are you frickin kidding me!

This is the best idea ever! Dudes now have a reason to stay in the strip club all night long Saturday. Yeah, honey…I'm just gonna' stick it out and wait til Church is over. This may be the first time in history a preacher passes the collection plate and yells DOLLA DOLLA BILLS, YA'LL. Now, the choir is gonna' sing a little Nickelback whilst you make it rain in this Temple of the Lord..and boobies.

Today, we're gonna' talk about the prostitute Mary Magdalene but I want this message to really sink in…so here to reenact the role of Mary Magdalene….Ya'll give a big church welcome to Cinnamon! As she shakes her moneymaker, I want you to imagine the temptation Jesus must have fought. Just look at those tassles spinning and listen to the clap clap clap of her badonkadonk. Oh look…more people who love the Lord coming in. Deacon Joe, could you go wipe down the VIP area to make room for this fine Christian family? You may need a mop. Come on, Pastor. I know the Bible teaches us to go where the sinners are but you can't have church in a place that smells like cigarettes, boob sweat and broken dreams. Jesus may be the most open minded being to ever walk the face of the Earth but even he didn't have disciples named Bubbles and Thumper. - PB

What if God Had a Facebook Page?

If God had a Facebook account, each day every human would receive another request from God to join "FarmVille", "Mafia Wars", "Happy Aquarium" or some other stupid waste of time. You would spend half your life clicking "Ignore", "Ignore", "Ignore" which would definitely put you in a precarious position since God does *not* like to be ignored.

Can you imagine logging in to your Facebook account and your homepage says:

"God poked you. Poke back?"

Mmm. That's a quandary: under any circumstances do you ever poke God? Is that a good idea? On one hand if you *don't* poke him he's going to think you don't care and you know what that means: 2,000 years of silence. On the other hand, if you *do* poke God you're going to come off as a little insolent because the first rule of social networking with God is:

Mortals Never Poke Deities!

Even if he pokes you first. So, I think the best answer is to *not* poke God and instead, send God a gift using "The Word of God" Facebook app.

You can never go wrong by bearing gifts as demonstrated by the Three Wise Men.

Sacrifice has always been a big plus in the eyes of God. Now, no one is suggesting you get all dead-lamb-on-the-alter crazy on God (at least not in this day and age) but then again, leaving an Arby's roast beef sandwich for the Lord is not exactly appropriate either. A good compromise might be a bushel of wheat. Wheat is a universal currency. You can eat it, you can bake it, you can barter with it, and you can appease the Lord with it. Oh, and a card is not necessary.

Just the bushel. – CD

The Balls Are in Her Court

A year ago, Ashley McIntyre decided to donate her kidney to a total stranger. Today, she's engaged to him, and their baby is due in June. "As soon as we started dating -- not long after that -- was when we realized, this was it," And on Christmas Day, after all the presents were opened, Danny Robinson pulled out one more gift: a small, wrapped box containing an engagement ring. He got down on one knee and asked her to marry him.

Are you frickin kidding me, dude! STOP RIGHT NOW! Have you thought this through at all? Maybe you needed a brain more than a kidney because you are on a bus with no brakes headed straight to tardville. And I know all of you are out there saying, how can you be mad at such a beautiful story? You see, before you hooked up, she DONATED a kidney. But as soon as you get married it becomes a trade. Her kidney for your balls. Because there is no possible way you can EVER win an argument. She's gonna' run up the credit cards and as soon as you start bitching she's gonna' say,

Oh I'm sorry. You don't think a few hundred dollars in new clothes is a fair trade for MY KIDNEY. They cut me open and took my kidney out and put it in your dying body. You see this scar? I can never wear a bathing suit again because I saved your life. I'm sorry if I wanna' cover it with Versace. Maybe we should both do returns. And I dare ya to try to work through it with booze. Oh, you blew out your kidney and now you wanna' pickle mine? Hell no. Now start my Fiat, we're headed to the mall. You may as well get you a shirt that says Ashley's Lil Mitch because she's gonna' saddle you up and ride you like Seabiscuit. Congratulations again on getting your kidney.

Oh, Happy Valentine's Day. - PB

The Truth is *Really* 'Out There'

My day job is doing a morning radio show. You can imagine how many different people I interact with everyday. Most are normal people. Some have purchased a one-way ticket on the crazy train and are hanging out the windows screaming at squirrels – and they contact us. This is a real, unedited email:

"I just wanted to say that I love you guys for playing all this music that is trying to get the truth out about Aliens and how fucked up our government is here in America. If it was not for radio stations like you all, then we would be up a shit creek... but I believe it is not too late for us here in America. Viva La Revolution of regaining our freedoms and exposing this truth about the alien presence. I think radio, the colbert report and john stewarts, and fox news need to just come out in the open about everything you all know to expose this once and for all. Fuck the law suits, that is what we are trying to change. Btw... through my research, and ya'll may not know this, the alien age weapons we are building here in America that we have been copying from the downed alien craft are being funded by drugs brought up from Mexico by an extensive system of people that have been in unison

175

for some time now... I believe it is why my cousin was killed. I am trying as hard as I can every day to get this message out, and even have a speech to give Friday.... I know ya'll keep hinting about aliens.... just go ahead and Say What You Know, TELL the PUBLIC!!!!!!   Please do this for us so that we can legalize pot, save the economy, and stop our evil government before Armageddon hits us full fledged, if we don't the rest of the world is going to team up and kick our fucking asses for what a few thousand government people are doing from shadows that citizens don't even know about. Tell everyone what the music means." – CD

'Pot' Still Legal for Lobsters

Let's establish one thing I think most of us could agree on: our groceries should not be alive - nor give the appearance of having a life - after they has been designated as food. The lone exception might be lobsters with their beady black eyes and known natural hatred for humans.

In January, 1905 *The Atlanta Constitution* reported that a famous chef died two days after being bitten by a lobster. Tragically, 25 years later in September 1930, a Boston jeweler named Samuel Friedman was killed by a lobster truck on State Street, according to *The Boston Herald*. Your honor, can you not see the pattern of these cruel-staceans?

Granted, I could only find evidence of two premeditated attacks by lobsters. Probably because I was forced to glean these facts from a free preview of two articles, courtesy of Google's archive function. Maybe if Rich Uncle Pennybags wasn't the only one who could afford the price of lobster, I wouldn't have to skimp on paying for my research and this book would be a better read for it.

Well, don't email me. Blame your precious lobsters.

IMHO, lobsters are pretty arrogant and probably deserve to be on death row right up until they get the "pot." But, not squids. God loved squids so much he gave them three hearts.

It's true. - CD

The Atlanta

Sunday, January 1905

Chef Dies From Lobster Bite

In January, 1905 The Atlanta Constitution reported that a famous chef died two days after being bitten by a lobster. Tragically, 25 years later in September 1930, a Boston jeweler named Samuel Friedman was killed by a lobster truck on State Street, according to The Boston Herald. Your honor, can you not see the pattern of these cruel-staceans?

Ren foll imp

The that rela the

Thanks to "Generators" on the Internet I Can Add Instant Credibility Without Actually Buying Copies of Original Documents. Suck It, Credibility.

A Short History of Yogurt

Yogurt has been around for about 5,400 years. No, not historically - I'm talking about that crap sitting in the back of your refrigerator with *mold*. Yogurt comes from a Turkish word that means "sissy food." Historians have traced the mention of yogurt back to some Turk named "Pliny the Elder." It wasn't the yogurt that helped him live so long. It was hope that kept Pliny going - hope that "Pliny the Wife" would cook him just one decent meal before he left this world instead of serving him yogurt night after night.

In olden Turkish times, there were no fruity Bravo-Channel flavors to make the yogurt tastier. So, the Turks flavored Pliny's yogurt with things like pig hooves, tree bark and dirt. Every once-in-a-while the Pliny household was able to get their hands on donkey sweat which was always a treat for that night's dinner serving of yogurt.

Donkey sweat: is there anything it can't do?

Anyway, Yogurt gained a name for itself as a medicinal substance when Francis I was suffering from severe diarrhea and none of the French doctors could help. A friend, *Suleiman the Magnificent* sent over a doctor friend and he cured Francis I with yogurt. When word got out - yogurt took off.

Today, the Yogurt Cartel (Dannon, Yoplait, Breyers and Light n' Lively) is still trying to convince us that their product will make and/or keep us regular. Dannon even hired actress Jamie Lee Curtis as a spokesperson for "Activia" yogurt. You remember Jamie Lee Curtis: the former "Scream Queen" who starred in such scary movies as *Halloween, The Fog, Prom Night* and *Terror Train.* Now, instead of *scaring* the shit out of you, she's gently *coaxing* it out with yogurt.

Activia contains something called "Bifidus Regularis." If you never want to eat another plate of food - including yogurt - then visit the Activia website and read about Bifidus Regularis. It's a name the marketing eggheads just made up! Dannon has even trademarked it.

Let me clarify: Bifidobacterium animalis is a bacteria found in the large intestines of most mammals including us. "Bifidus Regularis" is a trademark (a legal claim) on a specific subspecies strain of Bifidobacterium animalis called "DN 173010." Dannon is marketing that organism as "Bifidus Regularis".

This would be like researchers finding out that some red corpuscles in your blood looked like George Clooney and decided to market them as "Bloodicus Cloonaris"

Marketing is one of the most evil things in the world because it is amoral and without conscience. But, that's another book.

Now, if the yogurt makers *really* wanted men to buy their product they would make a few changes. For instance: they'd nix "Kiwi-Strawberry" in favor of "Bacon-Pork Rind" flavor. Instead of a little cup with a pathetically and pitiful amount of yogurt barely able to feed a starving child from a third-world country, they'd sell it in a container big enough to equal the mass and weight of a Whopper.

And design the container so it fits in a koozie.

Or better yet: sell it at convenience stores in big sizes. 7-11 has a drink called "The Big Gulp" and "Super Big Gulp." Maybe they could introduce a large serving of Bacon-Pork Rind yogurt called "The Big Cultured Slough" and "Super Big Intestinal Quagmire." Now you're talking. If I wanted itty-bitty kiddy cups of food, I'd go to the next dwarf convention in Las Vegas. – CD

Author Acknowledgement

If you liked this book, here are a couple of suggestions how to acknowledge that.

Recommend

Recommend the book. Post something about it on Facebook or Twitter! Tell a friend! Your words would mean a lot!

Review

Leave a positive review of the book on Amazon.com

Books by Corey Deitz:

Under the Popeye Rose (2015)
(Paperback, Kindle)

Time Prisoners (2013)
(Paperback, Kindle)

Zombie, D.C. (Shmit Happens) (2012)
(Paperback, Kindle)

Holy Shmit! (2012)
(Paperback, Kindle)

Shut Up! We All Have Issues! (2011)
(Paperback, Kindle)

The 2012 Guide Book or How to Make the End of the World Fun! (2009)
(Paperback, Kindle)

Vilified! Red Meat for Conservatives from a Guy Who's Got a Lot of Beefs (2009)
 (Paperback, Kindle)

Lessons from Camp: Wisdom in the Past Tents (2008)
(Paperback, Kindle)

The Cash Cage (2004)
(Kindle)

Available on Amazon.com in Kindle and Paperback

Made in the USA
Lexington, KY
12 December 2015